Table of Contents

Dedication v
Acknowledgments vii
About the Author..ix
Foreword xi

Chapter 1: We All Fall Down.....................................1
Chapter 2: Step 1 – Get Up.....................................15
Chapter 3: Step 2 – Putting It Back Together Again.........27
Chapter 4: Step 3 – The Antidote 41
Chapter 5: Step 4 – Version 2.0..............................55
Chapter 6: Step 5 – On Growth and Grief 69
Chapter 7: Step 6 – Make Your Bed!......................81
Chapter 8: Step 7 – Becoming Bullet Proof 93
Chapter 9: Step 8 – Giving Back 105
Chapter 10: Happy Re-Birthday! 115

*I dedicate this book to my mom,
Mariette Deschenes (February 27, 1942–March 16, 2015).
She was my strength here on earth and now from up above.
Happy birthday, Momma.*

To my daughter, Victoria, you inspire me every day to be a better woman. Please break lots of glass on your way to the top!

And also, to the only person to ever really know me, John Cusanelli, my best friend and the best father to our daughter Victoria.

Acknowledgments

To those who may never have known you made a difference in my life...

Victoria for being a kind, gentle and patient soul. You are a precious gift and all my strength comes from my love for you!

My mom and dad, I can't wait to see you in heaven, picking up where you left off.

John, my best friend and father of our wonderful daughter, thank you for your unconditional support and love.

La famiglia Cusanelli che per me sarà sempre famiglia. Naturalmente, in memoria di nonno che è con dio in paradiso. E nonna Vitangela, Domenic e Angela, Gabriel, Matteo, Emanuel, Serafino e Julie-Ann, Lucas e Kristopher.

Some of my greatest teachers and friends: Jimmy Kritikos, Jonathan and Liisa Denis, Marguerite Denis, Lorelei and Mark Anselmo, Wendy Shobe, Max Gibb, Mohamed Elhabiby, Mohamed Elseify, Noha Elsayed, Pat Moore, Rick Hanson, Dr. Lucy Miller, Craig Foley, Robyn Moser, Mike Shaikh, Filomena May, Rose and Manny Ferreirinha, Michael Barbero, Barliin Mohamed, Stephane Poirier, David Hancock, Hon. Ric McIver, Moe Amery, Janice Sarich, Manmeet Bhullar, Stephen Khan, Jim and Karen Prentice, Yvonne Fritz, Matt Jeneroux, David Xiao, Neil Webber, Kyle Fawcett, Dave Rodney, Dr. Neil

Acknowledgments

Brown, Jeff Johnson, Greg Weadick, Steve and Leanne Young, Stephan Mandel, Andreas Berko, Geoffrey Cann, Chad Ford, John Drummond, Michael Cooper, Derek Fildebrandt, Mike Ellis, Diana McQueen, Heather Klimchuck, David Dorward, Brent and Gail Shervey, Dr. Alan Chong, Patrick Higgerty, Christy Pierce, Tim Boston, Paul and Kathryn Pryce.

Those who continue to inspire my love of politics: The Right Honourable Stephen Harper and Laureen Harper, Jim Dinning, Gary Mar, Pierre and Ana Poilievre, Alan Hallman, George Sirois, Derek Ding, Danielle Smith, Jason Kenney, Heather Forsyth, and Pat Nelson.

All my University of Alberta, Beta Chi, Theta sisters for the days of carefree glory! And especially those who I've had the pleasure of staying connected with over the years.

To my paternal family, my beautiful grandmother, Uncle Greg, Aunt Dodie, Aunt Sue and Uncle Phil, Aunt Cindy and Uncle Rick, and my cousins in the South: I love you all, more than the miles that separate us!

Et à ma famille maternelle, merci d'avoir été mon rocher quand j'ai perdu ma mère. Je sais que vous êtes tous là pour m'encourager en son nom. Des gros bisous a vous tous mes cousins et cousines du coté Deschenes, mon oncle Charles et ma tante Angela, mon oncle Régis et mon oncle Maurice, mon oncle Raymond et ma tante Denise, ma tante Suzanne et mon oncle Rocky et ma tante Nicole et mon oncle Gilles.

About the Author

Christine Cusanelli was born in Kingston, Ontario, Canada. She was raised in Edmonton, Alberta and now lives in Calgary, with her daughter. She is an award-winning author, engaging public speaker, and she embodies the meaning of life-long learner. She is an avid scholar, with several degrees, including two master's degrees: an MA in psychology and an MBA.

No stranger to working hard to achieve her goals, Christine has been recognized by an Inspiration Award for her work as a business consultant, and during her time in public office, was awarded the prestigious Queen's Diamond Jubilee Medal for her significant contribution and achievement in community service. She is a fitness advocate, and has marathoner and triathlete to add to her repertoire of athletic achievements.

She served as an elected Member of the Legislative Assembly of Alberta and was appointed by the Premier of Alberta as a Cabinet Minister. Politics continues to be one of her passions, and she now owns a successful boutique consulting firm.

Christine is dedicated to the mission of empowering women leaders to unlock the door to the C-suite. Women CEOs and aspiring leaders seek her out for her unique expertise that includes using applied psychology and strategic business development. Her vision is to set more women up for success in a corporate world that continues to have a poor representation of women attaining and retaining positions

About the Author

of top leadership and top earnings. With more than 20 years of experience in organizational leadership, and having crashed through a few glass ceilings herself, Christine serves leaders who, like her, are outliers and believe that success is achieved on purpose.

Regarding her new book, Christine says "my goal in writing *100 Days to 100%* is to show everyone by my own example that our moments of greatest struggle are simply preparation for our greatest moments of growth. This way of looking at obstacles, whether they be personal or in business, opens avenues for everyone to turn setbacks into opportunities. Our setbacks actually make us more purposeful by requiring us to overcome obstacles and come back stronger and smarter."

Her own experiences of great success, followed by great disappointment, loss, and even outright failure, offer readers comfort and insight, as well as hope. Never one to get counted out of the game, Christine personifies the *meaning* of smashing the glass ceiling and never giving up, no matter the trials.

If you would like to invite Christine to speak or consult with your organization, please contact her at christine@RenewYourPurposeToday.com or visit her book site at RenewYourPurposeToday.com.

You can also follow her on:
Facebook https://www.facebook.com/ConsultChristine/
Instagram https://www.instagram.com/consultchristine/
LinkedIn https://www.linkedin.com/in/consultchristine/

Foreword

100 Days to 100% is a refreshingly practical set of steps that will take you from helpless to hopeful. I am familiar with Christine's ability to achieve whatever she sets her mind to, so rest assured that you are in for an amazing transformation. Besides being an award-winning author, Christine is no stranger to high achievement. She is an athlete and scholar with multiple degrees, and she has already changed tens of thousands of people's lives as a principal and an elected legislator. She has even served in one of the highest-ranking political offices as a Cabinet Minister. She knows what great success is, but she also knows a thing or two about the humility that it takes to gain success, as well as the possible pitfalls.

Christine's approach to renewing your purpose will transform your current thinking and teach you a mindset that will magically inspire you to level up by discovering the special reason for which you were put on earth. What a priceless gift!

What happens when you find yourself experiencing a dark night of the soul moment, and you don't know if the light at the end of the tunnel is another oncoming train? Christine articulates, through this book, a life-changing strategy, and gently but assuredly guides you to a new, greater path of freedom and success. Whether it be personal or business, the path that leads to freedom is found by truly knowing what makes you feel alive! Your PURPOSE.

Achieving greatness has everything to do with getting back up again. Christine's 8 Steps will teach you not only *how* to get back up,

Foreword

but also how to create your own personal antidote to the little and not so little upsets that are just part of life. Because really, you know that without darkness, there is no light, don't you?

You are about to meet yourself again for the first time. I invite you to enjoy this journey of *100 Days to 100% - 8 Steps to Renew Your Purpose!*

Raymond Aaron
New York Times Bestselling Author

Chapter 1
We All Fall Down

*"So go ahead. Fall down.
The world looks different from the ground."*
– Oprah Winfrey

1

Think about walking past a park or a gathering of young children. Imagine what you see. What do you hear? Probably kids running at full speed ahead to get onto the slide, or chasing each other and calling out, "You're it!" They are in full glee as they enjoy their play. You may remember the children's nursery rhyme, in most parts of the world, called "Ring a Ring of Roses." It goes something like this:

> "Ring-a-ring-a-roses,
> A pocket full of posies,
> A-tishoo! A-tishoo!
> We all fall down."

It matters not what version you sang as a child. It doesn't matter the origin of the verses or even who wrote it. Here's what matters. You see, when children gather hands and begin to chant the words together in song, they race around in a joined circle, as fast as they possibly can. They giggle and outright laugh. They skip and are elated to holler out the song as loudly as possible.

Then, at the end of the song, what happens? Do you remember doing this as a child? If not, I will tell you. Everyone races to be the first to fall down! All the children race to fall down and roll on the ground, laughing and watching their friends fall to the ground too. And what happens to the last person to fall down? They are excluded from the next round of the game and have to sit out. No more falling down and rolling around having fun for them; they have to sit on the park bench and wait until their friends are satisfied that they've fallen down enough to move on to another game!

What's the point, you ask? Think about how we embraced falling down as kids. We were free and unencumbered from the responsibilities and the accountability that we carry when things fall down as adults. We are fed the belief, day in and day out, that things must go up: the stock market, our upward climb for a promotion up the corporate ladder. . . We even give a thumbs up for approval. You get the point. We are socialized to be afraid to fall down, and to be ashamed of our failures. We avoid mistakes at all costs; some even avoid action as a means to keep themselves from falling. They become driven by fear, which accumulates in their mindset and causes anxiety, depression, and compulsive disorders.

And what of those people who show bravery, take risks, and while well intended, something goes wrong and they find themselves benched, in the penalty box, fired, CANCELLED? How do they get up?

If this sounds scary, it is. I know; I've been there. And what I've learned from falling down is that getting back up is about who you ARE, not what you've done. And yes, that also means "who you are" is not the title or the credentials or the money you successfully earned, any more than it is the scandal on the front page, the job you lost, the marriage that didn't work out, or the business that collapsed.

Who you ARE is a human, "being" on earth to know yourself better than anyone else knows you. The surprise is that knowing who you ARE means first knowing who you are not. And most of the time—I have to be completely transparent with you—we learn that the hard way. Think about the most famous people in the world who have achieved great things. Did you know that Walt Disney was fired because apparently his editor at the Kansas Daily Star thought he had no imagination? That editor nearly ruined all of our chances to experience the "happiest place on earth!" I mean, what if Mr. Disney actually believed he wasn't the uber creative genius who changed the course of how we see love, through Ariel's willingness to sacrifice; and feel compassion towards animals like Simba, because of Scar? Disney theme park would never have become the "Magical Kingdom" if Walt Disney believed that he had no imagination. I'm sure you agree that it's hard to imagine a world without the work of Disney. And that's why it's so important that we know ourselves well. Because, in the real world, people are going to try to tell you who you are not, and you have to be able to stand your ground on who you ARE.

Which leads me to a very basic but fundamental question for you. It is the raison d'etre of this book! When you figure out who you ARE, you can find your purpose.

What does purpose mean to you?

Is it having a lot of money? No judgement here! It's okay to want to have a comfortable life. Is it having a happy family? A good marriage, or giving to your community? Maybe for you, purpose is your spiritual connection. Maybe you live for helping the vulnerable, and want your legacy to be about leaving this earth a little better than you found it. Finding your purpose will lead you to moments of unimaginable glory, wins, love, grace, and peace. If it seems elusive or unattainable from your perspective right now, that's okay because, guess what? It's going through that kind of doubt that leads you to your next great "aha!"

This is what my book is going to show you how to do: find your purpose from the place you're at now, and show you how to guard it against being extinguished by the challenges of life. I think you already know that those challenges aren't going to end just because you discover your purpose. The good news that I can tell you, from my own experience and learning from others, is that when you know who you are and what your purpose is, there is little that can get in the way of your success. And perhaps right now, you are experiencing someone who has challenged your knowledge of who you are; perhaps you've made a major mistake that goes completely against the values you possess. Or maybe you feel you've been treated unfairly and that the odds are against you. But here is the deal: There is no light without darkness. And in the same way that light can only exist because of the dark, you can only discover who you ARE by being challenged to determine who you are NOT.

As for the 100 days to 100%, the choice is up to you. I believe that if you implement these 8 Steps with clarity, honest intention, dedication and most of all with discipline, you experience a brand new perspective. That change is, of course, not going to end at the 100 day mark, but you will have made a major dent in the work that is required to get you on your way to living a meaningful life that is aligned with your purpose. Also, 100% is something that I'd like you to consider a benchmark rather than a target. It serves little purpose to invest in the false belief that we can be 100% all the time. But, at the core of this 8 step process, is being mindful of hitting that 100% mark time and time again in between moments of reflection, resistance and outright denial. These are parts of life's journey after all!

I'd like to share an example of this from my own life. At the very least, you'll realize you're in good company of someone who has hit her own rock bottom—a number of times! And I know that I'll hit a few more before my time on earth is up. It's taken me a really long time to get to this place of reality; so, if you're not here yet, don't worry. What's more, I'm learning that our purpose changes, gets clearer, and evolves with every adjustment—sometimes those that are forced on us, and especially those we accept. We're never finished the discovery of purpose; it's like a beautiful painting that every time you see it in different lighting or from varying perspectives, it changes your experience of it and its *meaning* to you.

My latest example of this is life after politics. Growing up, my parents were always involved political party members. I remember them dragging me along to meetings, and even though I was supposed to do my homework while the board discussed "important party business," I was always drawn into the animation of these meetings. I was about 8 years old, sitting with my math book and perfectly sharpened pencil, along the wall in the back of the room. It never really mattered to me that I couldn't comprehend what the discussion was all about. The excitement of the people in the room was magnetic! I was glued to the debate like it was the last episode of *Friends*, or maybe today's last episode of a Netflix series. People were ignited in discussion, sometimes even shouting! I wondered what they could be so upset about. It was the gateway to my interest in politics.

When I was 12 years old, a local candidate paid me five dollars an hour to sell memberships to the party over the phone. I also dropped flyers in mailboxes, and recorded voter information by going door to door. I was hooked. Being a girl, I didn't really see a future for myself in politics; that came later as a sudden commitment that was fulfilled by the universe. At work one day, in a lively discussion about political values, I said aloud to two of my colleagues that I was going to become the Minister of Education one day. I said it to them in a tone of jest, but inside of me, I meant it. Within a year and a half of that sudden proclamation, I was appointed as the Minister of Tourism, Parks, and Recreation. So, when I tell you that there is little that can stop you from succeeding when you know yourself and your purpose, it wasn't just me trying to hand you a pair of rosy coloured glasses. Things magically happen when you put those two things together. It's like making fire—all you need is the tinder and the flint.

Now, that was a lot of magic to make happen in one shot. I'm still in awe of how the universe just lit up that path for me to find my way. And you may be annoyed to hear that I've done things like this all my life. Don't get down on yourself and start beating yourself up with statements like, "I'm so unlucky," or "That never happens for me," because I want to share my strategy with you—BUT—it comes with a warning. Here on earth, what goes up, must come down. So, besides sharing with you how to go up, I feel it's my responsibility to show you also what to do when you come down.

On May 5, 2015, it was the end of my own "up." In what I can only describe as a political blood bath, the governing party of Alberta, which had reigned for 44 years straight, fell. And I fell too. Hard. Of the 87 legislature seats, the governing party held 70 going into the election. Our historic loss was epic. We lost 62 seats and became the third-place party. No one had ever lived and worked in an Alberta run by any other government; and most of us, whether we won or lost our seats, were shunned from even our own supporters. Or that's how it felt. Members returning to previous careers shared stories about the difficulties of fitting in. Some couldn't find work because the stigma of being a fallen politician was coupled with anger towards the government for winning those 44 years, and also, for losing.

For me personally, it was the darkest period of my life, which seemed to drag on for years. The slow descent began weeks before the election writ was dropped. My mom, my best friend and rock, died unexpectedly. My heart was broken. I was in a state of shock, but I had to proceed. I was so traumatized by this loss that I can barely remember that 40-day period. I don't even know if I cared that I lost. But I was in pain. I was in a lot of pain, and I was scared. I tried to put on a smile and a stiff upper lip, as my mother would say, but in the months that passed, I made many mistakes that all amounted to my inability to get back up quickly. And when I thought I could get up, I was hit with more waves of disappointment, and more loss, to the point that I didn't think I could take it anymore. I planned how to kill myself.

I now know some very important, factual elements that play a huge role in moments like my post-political ride through hell. The body's response to loss, for example, is very much the same kind of response that can be triggered by trauma. This is a topic that is being discussed pervasively throughout society, and thankfully so. Trauma is caused by a disturbing event, perceived or real, that causes us to fear for our physical safety, our lives, our livelihood. Now, you can't judge another person for their ability or inability to mitigate their psychological or physiological response to a traumatic event. Imagine an empty glass. Imagine that empty glass is your life. As a child, you fall down the stairs and break your arm. Fill the glass about an inch from the bottom. The incident, like the water, remains in the glass. A major event occurs, like the death of a sibling—add more water to the glass, filling it about a quarter from the bottom. Then add other events that fill the glass, without emptying it in between. Eventually, the glass flows over with water. Trauma is like that. Your central nervous system adapts by triggering adrenalin, cortisol, and other hormones that are meant to help us flee the situation or be on alert for similar events. The thing is that sometimes, an event causes the central nervous system to get stuck in high gear. The water keeps flowing and spilling over the rim of the glass. You start to feel symptoms of stress, like anxiety attacks, exhaustion, or obsessing about things and trying to get some control over your seemingly chaotic situation. This turns into anger, bitterness, and impatience with others. You start to underperform at work, you blame people around you, and no one seems to understand what you've been through—and worse, no one can help you feel any better.

ALL of this is normal. I'm telling you this because it's all part of the process of getting up, which is Step 1. You really have to understand that you've fallen, and that getting up is going to take an admission on your part that the world looks different when you're sitting on the ground bruised and broken. This means admitting that you need to heal your central nervous system, which should include advice from your physician. What's more, if you try to fake your way through it, you will take longer to recover. The choice is yours. Personally, I prefer getting to the end point as quickly as possible. But I'll be honest; that's not what I did.

Believe me when I say that 100 Days to 100% is not of this earthly plane. Even, failure has a purpose. Its purpose is to cause your complete surrender. If you're anything like me, you resist surrendering at every cost. For years, in my journey to renewing my own purpose after my epic political loss, I resisted dealing with being taken down. I did many things (which I will share in this book) that prolonged my pain and agony, even though I know now that I was getting all kinds of nudges to surrender and take care of the grief and loss I was experiencing. When my mom died, the universe quietly whispered to me to drop out of the race, by sending a very mean messenger. A political operative from one of the other parties threatened to expose a sad but juicy scandal involving my family. I had just lost my mother, and this scandal would plaster intimate details about my father and the dysfunction that is part of my and every family. I could barely hold it together to campaign each day, and I was ready to quit. That was a sign for me to surrender, but I refused to take it. I was stubborn, and even though I could see this downward spiral, I felt like I had to hold on. I think I was destined to hit the pavement really hard. It was as though everything was perfectly orchestrated for me to fail, and the ensuing mistakes I made, when I landed face first, were each cultivated out of my spirit's need to level up.

I was being asked to shed the parts of my ego that prevented me from finding my purpose. Those parts were stubbornness, vanity, hatred, anger, pride, selfishness, and a whole lot of other great descriptive words to basically tell me that I had lost my way. I refused to accept these as being a part of my resistance to surrendering. It took many more painful attempts by the universe to try to coax my surrender. I had 3 car accidents, physical injuries leading to surgery, lost friendships, horrible job experiences, and even the tragic and unexpected deaths of friends that I cherished. I was brought to my knees and to the floor, again and again, for about 4 years. You see, I refused to surrender. I refused to let go of rigid paradigms, practices, and routines. You'll read in Steps 5 and 6 about these three, and about the importance of establishing behaviours that are aligned with your purpose as a means to rebuild and create your own personal antidote that will help you weather the storms, no matter how strong.

And if you're a skeptic about how car accidents and injuries could be messages to provoke my surrender, just read up on postulation, which can be used to manifest abundance by casting out a declaration to the universe. If I believe that I could manifest my own appointment to Cabinet, and I do, there is no doubt in my mind that I can create havoc using the exact same principle of postulation. I'll discuss postulation later, but suffice to say for now, it is powerful and can be used for good and bad. In Step 8, you'll read about postulation and also about some of the neurological research that supports why cognitive patterns are critical to our mental health and well-being. But suffice to say, embracing "failure" and its best friend, "mistakes," is something that you will look at from a completely new lens at the end of this book. This is because your ability to surrender your ego completely, and examine your failures and mistakes, will lead directly to the discovery of your purpose. And when you meet your purpose again in the upgraded version of yourself, as I told you already, there will be very little, if anything, that can get in the way of your success.

Now, I don't want to end the very first chapter of my very first book on a downer. I don't share any of these experiences with you to make you feel sorry for me because life isn't fair. Sometimes life isn't fair. So what.

Let me go back to the Lion King topic that I began this chapter with. Even if you've never seen the *Lion King* movies or Broadway musical, you'll likely have some recollection of the music composed for it: "Circle of Life," "Hakunamatata," or "I Just Can't Wait to Be King." You're probably singing those songs in your head now!

Hans Zimmer, who wrote the film's musical score pieces, including "Life's Not Fair," shares a poignant message during an interview he did about his decision to work on *The Lion King*. This example will drive home the point about fairness in life.

We All Fall Down

So, Zimmer is a pretty accomplished guy. He is known for his work on movies, like *The Dark Knight*, *Gladiator*, and *Inception*. In his interview, he tells the host that he didn't want to work on *The Lion King*. He thought Disney pictures would expect superficial music without depth. He refused, at first. Of his experience, he said that "the wrong decisions always take you on a great adventure." He actually decided to write the music because, at the time, his daughter was 6 years old. He wanted to show off to her, and admits that he took the job to be able to bring her to the premiere! How's that for making a decision based on the wrong reason. But is it? What he discovered in the process was that making music for *The Lion King* was not just about animals. The story is about a son losing his father.

Zimmer could immediately empathize with this, as he had lost his own father when he was very young. He'd always felt as though this just wasn't fair. He had never fully dealt with his father's death, and he found himself transforming the grief and loss into a requiem to his father, through what is today one of the most successful Disney movies. I imagine he regretted the initial decision and begrudgingly began to compose its music, and soon recognized the tap on his shoulder—perhaps a nod from the other side—to not only honour the memory of his father but also produce a legacy for his daughter. Not to mention the millions who watched and were moved by his musical composition, perhaps to their own catharsis. If you'd like to watch this interview, it's available on my website: RenewYourPurposeToday.com.

And here's some more good news. Eventually, when you get to the point of realizing that what you've done really doesn't matter at all, it's a tremendously freeing experience. What I mean by this is that what we do is simply the vehicle to fulfill our purpose. Sometimes we get it wrong and we are forced to surrender, and we must listen and watch very carefully for the signs that we are aligned once again with our purpose. And when this alignment comes together, the experience is a feeling. It feels like when you're driving on the highway, singing at the top of your lungs, with the music blasting in your car. And if you've never shamelessly sang your way from Calgary to Edmonton, maybe you can identify with the feeling of jumping up and down when your favourite hockey team scores the winning goal, or your child completes her first dance solo on pointe shoes, or you receive the news that your tests are cancer free.

Your touch stone to that feeling is the beginning of renewing your purpose. Before you move on to the next chapter on how to find your way up again, I want you to do something very important. Set a timer; take five minutes to sit in a quiet spot. Flip through the files in your memory until you stop at one of those moments where you felt completely free. Recall the elation, laughter, the full breath that you inhaled and exhaled, the sun warming your skin or the cool breeze brushing your cheeks. You will feel that again, and even more. Let's get on with it!

Chapter 2
Step 1 – Get Up

"Sometimes when you innovate, you make mistakes. It is best to admit them quickly, and get on with improving your other innovations."
– Steve Jobs

2

Did you know that the Earth is pulling you down? No, really, it is. Newton's third law in physics has proven that the Earth is pulling you down with a gravitational force of 500 N (N stands for Newtons, which is essentially a measurement of weight). Our bodies are also miraculously pulled upward with the same force, so this makes a perfect balance, not to mention that it keeps you from floating away by pulling you towards the Earth. You've of course heard of the expression, "what goes up, must come down." We don't know that Sir Isaac Newton actually said this, but it sure is a good rule to keep in mind. You see, I think it's nature's way of evening out the playing field. It doesn't matter who you are or where you're from, we've all got the same chance to fall as we do to rise.

Basically, in the laws of physics, every action has an equal and an opposite reaction. Applied philosophically, this means that moments of elation are going to be followed by deflation. There is obviously good news and bad news about this. I'll start with the bad news to get that out of the way. Yes, you will fail. Yes, you will make mistakes, get it wrong, and screw it up, and you'll find yourself having varying degrees of failing, depending sometimes on the level of risk you take. But don't stop taking risks! Don't stop trying to get it right. Why take a risk if it's going to lead to failure, you ask? Well, this leads to the good news. And that is that mistakes and failures allow us time to reboot. During that period of time when all seems lost, this is your moment to look at the world from a whole new perspective. It's easy to get into a tailspin when this happens. You panic and try scrambling to get up. Don't. That's not how you get back up.

Step 1 – Get Up

Remember how I said figuring out who you are is often found by learning who you are not? Well, getting up works similarly. And if you are ready to go on the journey to figuring out your purpose, then buckle up, because it sometimes feels like being a cowboy during bull riding finals at the rodeo. If you've never been to a rodeo, let me explain. A cowboy is scored on his ability to stay on the bull for a full 8 seconds; and beyond that, depending on how hard the bull is bucking, and on the cowboy's ability to hold on tight, with a little finesse too, he can win the money prize, a fantastically gawdy belt buckle and some damn good bragging rights. Getting up is just like a bull ride, minus maybe the fantastically gawdy belt buckle. The most important part about getting up is this: HOLDING ON. The wilder the ride, the higher the score you'll likely get, but that 8 seconds is going to seem like the longest 8 seconds ever.

Holding on means that you have to respect that you've been taken down. You've got to be a good sport about it too. If you blame others for your mistakes, you are absolutely missing the point, and you will prolong your fall to the ground. I can promise you that 100%. And here's the other reality check that you need to get your whole body and mind to believe. Do not become a victim. It's a trap that will pull you further down, and it will only give off the impression that you lack humility. You're going to need humility (more on that later). Let me explain, because this is very important. Life is not fair. It's never going to be fair and, all around us, there are people who are struggling to prove this point. The only fairness in it is that we all get our turn to struggle. But do not focus on who treated you badly, who scammed you, what bad luck you've had, or any other excuse that will keep you from taking this golden opportunity to learn from falling down. Yes, this is all on you. And if you think someone is going to come and offer you a line or a hand up—or worse, if you believe you are entitled to it—you're going to take a long time to rise.

Look, I know that's not the kind of gentle, easy, and pretty advice you may have hoped to find when you opened up this book. But if you aren't ready for the realities of getting up from a bad fall, then close the book and go back to what you were doing before.

Still here? Good. I'm glad. I want you to regain your ground and feel powerful again. But I'm not going to lie to you either. First, I'm a terrible liar, and second, what you're going to learn by following the 8 steps, will work if you follow them exactly as I tell you. I've done this a number of times, and if you have a look at all that I've achieved in between getting swatted to the ground, it's proof that what I have done works. I have the financial freedom and abundance to travel, enjoy the comforts of a luxury home, drive a luxury car, and splurge—my daughter has everything a 20-something-year-old could ever need or want. I work every day on building better relationships, loving myself, and treating myself with kindness and forgiveness. All of these gifts have been worked for by being honest with myself in those times when life seemed like crap. I have dug really deep in those times to get real with myself, so that I could truly understand how I took the path that led me away from my purpose. It's YOUR choices that lead YOU down the wrong path to finding yourself face first in the dirt.

So, get real with yourself right now. Did you take that job, which you now hate, for the right reasons, or was it because you were padding your ego? Are your relationships failing because you aren't able to give to others when it feels like they aren't giving to you? Are you drinking or taking drugs because you want to avoid thinking or feeling like you don't belong, or because you're more fun, more relaxed, and more focused? Are you unable to connect with your child because you are stuck in your own past? Are your finances in a mess because you've made bad decisions and you're embarrassed? I could actually go on about the many ways we stray from our purpose. But the point is that it is time that you do something to help yourself get up. No one else can do it for you.

Getting real is the first thing you have to do. It's going to hurt too. I'm sorry to tell you that, but I promise that what waits beyond the

Step 1 – Get Up

pain of your own truth is the most beautiful feeling you can have on earth. I'm going to be real with you about one truth that I learned about myself, which if I did not admit, would never have allowed me to get up.

I'm sad and embarrassed about it, and I wished at first that I didn't have to look at it, because it's ugly. But now that I've forgiven myself, I have found this amazing path to freedom that feels like swimming in a river and being pulled in the right direction by the flow of crisp, clear waters.

Listen, I don't need to tell you how nasty the political world can be. You've seen how politicians get treated. I've seen how politicians treat each other. I have never been in a more vicious pool of sharks than that. It didn't take long for me to get swept up into that same way of treating others. When I look back, I was in a trance of kill or be killed. For a long time I was so ashamed of the blood that was on my hands. I have secrets that I've never told anyone, and I will take them to my grave. But I have admitted to myself that being cut-throat, mean, and lacking compassion for my enemies is not part of my character. I was going against my purpose in every way, and the proof was in the failures that I experienced as a result of those mistakes. When in politics, exacting revenge and standing back to watch someone's house burn down at my hands didn't phase me. It does today. And when I took responsibility for my actions, forgave myself, and truly let go of that horrible part of my life, I began to heal.

Today, I still have to remind myself that I'm forgiven by the universe. I followed a path that led me to pain. I had full control over that. Today, I have gotten up from the fall along that path by realizing that my purpose is to see the light, rather than the darkness, in others. I've built a successful consulting practice on this, and I help business executives discover their purpose, because I know mine: I am a seeker of light. I see light in people, and I can find the light through the darkness. That's my gift and my calling. I help people unlock and unleash potential in their business because I've learned that there is darkness and chaos and evil around us, and we should be aware of it. But more importantly, there is light and goodness, order and abundance. When I focus on that, the light grows stronger and stronger. Step 1 is this: When you make mistakes and fall, stop and listen. It's your chance to get up and be stronger than ever. Your task is to first believe that little voice inside of you, which is telling you, "I gave you this challenge for a reason." No matter if your belief comes from the universe, God, your cognition, or whatever, the message is this: "I see that you have the potential to get through it. Get up."

Get up. That's the first step. So, how are you going to get the courage to take this step? First, you need to know that it's going to take time. You can only speed up the process if you are truly ready for the work. I mean truly dedicated. You can lie to yourself, but the forces of nature won't be fooled. Don't try to take a shortcut, or you'll simply start clipping along what you think is the right path, only to find it doesn't lead to the Emerald City; it leads to the Dark Forest. But don't be scared if this happens. The road to freedom has a map. Actually, there are lots of maps. I'm going to tell you what worked for me. Give it a try.

What I've discovered is that when we make mistakes, especially big mistakes, we've actually lost ourselves. Let me explain. Mistakes happen most often when we aren't paying attention, when we lose sight of our values, when we're tired, when we're emotional, and so on. The state we're in causes us to stray from our main purpose. Think about it. If you've been unable to sleep, you might be unable to concentrate at work. This could cause you to have an accident if you're working at a job involving physical labour, or to make an error in judgement if you're leading an organization. To fulfill your purpose, as I will show you in Steps 4 and 6, you must be equipped with strong practices, habits, and routines. It all goes together in a sort of synergy. When we stray from our path and find ourselves in the Dark Forest, we've lost this *meaningful* synergy. The ensuing consequences can be

Step 1 – Get Up

mild and easily corrected, and you can return to your path. But when a major catastrophe strikes, and the consequences are severe, you get benched and actually go through the stages of GRIEF. Grief doesn't just strike when you lose a loved one to death. It's also a very real part of getting back up.

I encourage you to read up on the stages of grief, a theory developed by Dr. Elisabeth Kübler-Ross. You'll see yourself in these stages, and it will be comforting. These are explained in Kübler-Ross's book, *On Death and Dying*. The stages are denial, anger, bargaining, depression, and acceptance.

I bring up Dr. Kübler-Ross's work here because Step 1 is all about getting real and working on denial. There are three main tasks that go along with being accountable and not getting caught up in denying your situation.

- Take time to yourself.
- Find 2 confidantes.
- Get help.

Taking time to yourself is something that you will have trouble with at first. If you look into Dr. Kübler-Ross's stage called denial, you'll see that it is characterized by avoidance, confusion, elation, shock, and fear. I'm not going to go into these at any great depth, but it's worth pointing this out so that you can consciously reflect on it. This is because if you want to get on the path to renewing your purpose, you're going to need to take the time to quiet your mind and body to be able to learn from your mistakes. Remember when I mentioned that your central nervous system responds to trauma in a physiological way? Well, this is likely happening when you start Step 1. You're probably not thinking straight either. So, if it's possible, take a trip, preferably alone, to somewhere relaxing. Don't do a travel adventure. This is not the time for that. You need to sleep—a lot. Also, you need to reduce the stimuli around you so that your body can start to calm down.

www.RenewYourPurposeToday.com

I chose to go to Hawaii when I was removed from Cabinet. It was a major adjustment to get used to being fired and then seeing it all over the front pages of the newspaper. I was assured by the premier that this was just a normal part of service and not to worry, and that I'd be in Cabinet again. She gave no rationale, and I felt all of the emotions I just mentioned. I avoided feeling sad, and acted outwardly strong; I was confused about how to deal with this as I had been a high-flyer throughout my career. I was shocked to see how the media tore me to shreds and insulted my character on the front page of the news, chasing me down the halls of the legislature to try and catch me in an awkward pose for photos and video. I felt like I had been used as a gladiator fighting lions to his death. It took me years to fully recover from this and, today, I proudly bear the scars I feel I earned. Through these words, I unburden myself completely and tell you that I have atoned for my own mistakes, and have forgiven myself and others. If I had not been able to do that, I would still be in a state of chaos, blindly searching for what my heart desires. I no longer fear failing. I still work at not beating myself up when I make mistakes, but I know that failure is just God's way of telling me that something isn't aligned.

So, back to Hawaii. I took my daughter so she wouldn't have to listen to the news or have students at her school make hurtful comments. Maybe it would blow over in a couple of weeks. It did not. But we slept in, sat in the hot tub overlooking the ocean, ate the most delicious tuna poke, and took surfing lessons. While I took those lessons, I realized how much physical strength I had lost. Politics is very bad for your health. You sit a lot and go from event to event and meeting to meeting. Because you're greeting people all the time, you eat a piece of shrimp cocktail here and a little puff pastry there. I was a runner when I got into politics. I had run marathons and done triathlons. My physical health was just one aspect that I would have to reckon with. Getting up on that surfboard was hard. But not as hard as the journey that would follow to finally arrive at this point of freedom and success that I have today. It's not easy getting up. But it's worth it.

Step 1 – Get Up

The next two things that are absolutely necessary to help you get up, go together. You're going to need help, and it's going to have to come from sources that can show unconditional love. This is not as easy as you might think. It might not be your significant other, and this may surprise and disappoint you. Try not to be hard on your friends and loved ones. They may not have the skills to help you effectively. That can't be helped. So, choose wisely. I suggest a spiritual advisor, an elder, or someone who is not directly involved in the challenge you're trying to overcome. The reason I say this is because, when you spend time with this person, they may be able to offer you a fresh perspective, and are not so close to the issue that they carry their own feelings of anger or loss. The best thing to do is make a regular coffee date with this person, just as you would with anyone else. Don't tell them you'd like them to be your confidante either. Let the relationship take form organically. You don't need to talk about your current situation. You just need to begin surrounding yourself with good people.

Be careful about your attitude during this time of renewal. You should aim to build two new confidantes, and you will probably recognize that many of your old friends and loved ones seem to disappear. This hurts, but people are not trying to be mean. The fact is that most people don't like conflict. You may be in a rough place, and that's scary for you. But you know what? It's scary for others to see you in that place. Most people want to be able to fix something easily. And your friends and loved ones also instinctively know that you cannot be fixed by them. Think about when an emergency happens, and an ambulance needs to be called. There is always the person who runs to the scene and is comfortable taking the lead. But those people are much fewer than those who stand by watching, or those who slowly shake their heads and walk away. Some people just can't handle seeing others in pain.

And think about what happens when the ambulance is called. The person who takes the lead helps triage the patient to the emergency responders, and the patient is taken to get professional help. The leader is the type of confidante you're looking for. They will be steadfast, they will follow through, they are selfless, and most importantly, they are compassionate. Do not fall into the trap of choosing someone you think is your closest friend if they don't fit those qualities. I'm telling you this because if you do, they will disappoint you; and right now, that is the last thing you need. They won't do it on purpose, but if you're good friends with someone who is a lot of fun to hang around with, yet whenever you make a plan to meet, they are late or cancel—or worse, don't show up—don't expect them to change just because you're facing a crisis. And if you try to force this point, you will become angry and frustrated, and may very well not be able to keep yourself from responding badly.

From my own experience, when we're in a crisis, our senses are on overdrive. Our emotions are too. If you want to keep your friendships from deteriorating, it is best to set some very well-defined boundaries for your own interactions with others. You may not realize it, but your responses are likely way more emphasized than normal, and this can really make others uncomfortable. If you want to maintain your friendships, really watch your interactions, and try to be mindful of this. And when you make a mistake and get angry or emotional, call that friend as soon as possible to apologize. They may or may not forgive you, but you are still doing the right thing by your character so that, at the very least, you can forgive yourself.

Lastly, and back to the topic of that patient who was triaged to the right medical help, you need to find an excellent physician. They will be your saving grace in so many ways. I happened to have a wonderful family physician who has seen me through each wave that pulled me into the many undercurrents I've survived. Your doctor needs to be personable first. If you don't like them on a personal level, I'm telling you to find one that you do. When you visit your physician, you should feel as though you have a qualified professional who treats you unconditionally and without prejudice. There's no room for judgement right now. So, if you need to shop around for the right profes-

Step 1 – Get Up

sional, make this a priority. They will be a major asset on your journey and can act as your advocate when you need it, your mirror when you need to hear how you've improved, and most of all, the trained professional who works every day with patients just like you. They have a wealth of knowledge that can help you feel normal, and they can reassure you that what you are going through is common and survivable. It's also important to be honest with your physician, because they can get you help for your physical and mental health related issues. You don't have to suffer behind a mask of strength. Getting medical advice will be a major factor in your being able to get back up after a fall.

You've mastered Step 1 when you're able to be real with yourself, accept your situation as being a challenge that is not permanent, and have surrounded yourself with people who can provide important comfort and guidance. Having this in place will give you a running start on Step 2. You're going to be putting your life back together again. Soon, you're going to be able to see yourself growing and changing into a person of renewed strength and new wisdom. From there, a manifestation of new ideas and opportunities that you didn't believe were possible will begin to appear.

Chapter 3
Step 2 – Putting It Back Together Again

"To all those who have suffered as a consequence of our troubled past, I extend my sincere thoughts and deep sympathy. With the benefit of historical hindsight, we can all see things which we would wish had been done differently or not at all."
– Queen Elizabeth II

3

You live in a world that glorifies perfection. It's everywhere around you. If you live in North America (and even if you don't), Disney has most likely formed a big part of the joy and essence of your childhood, where movies, family vacations, and books were a part of your everyday life. I started to realize that I rejected the message that Disney promoted to me growing up, right around the time my marriage wasn't working. You see, most girls grow up believing that Prince Charming is going to come along and swoop them off their feet to "happily ever after." When I got married in my early twenties, I thought so too. How could I help it? Disney has done such a good job selling to us all! Don't get me wrong; I still love the magic of Disney, but I also have learned not to get caught up in the idealism of this message as well. It's not my fairy godmother who is going to come and help me avenge the ugly stepsisters. I've learned that my faith, truth, discipline, and compassion is what sees me through tough times.

By the way, when I mention faith or God in this book, feel free to go with whatever your beliefs are, be they agnostic, new age, religious, or spiritual. The point is, we've all been living by certain paradigms that are tested in tough times. It's of no use to compare our lives to the characters we see in movies. To be honest, I believe that this is actually a form of propaganda. I'm not saying it's a bad thing to enjoy Disney, but let's be realistic about this. We are being sold merchandise, fairy tales, and ideals that suit the promotion of the free market. It's essential that we promote free enterprise for thriving economies, peace in society, and promoting hope in people. It's really no different

Step 2 – Putting It Back Together Again

than other ideological messaging. I've lived in China. President Xi has traded in "communism" for what he calls "socialism with Chinese traits." The focus is the same no matter the name. One party rule and military order is President Xi's mission, and he's named himself leader for life to be sure of that. I'm not a proponent of one party systems, but I also don't blindly ignore that the West achieves order, peace, and prosperity through advertising, public messages, and education. We like to think we are living in the free world. And for the most part, we are; but advertising, art, and culture are all directed at asking us to fill a certain paradigm in society: grow up, get married, have children, work, retire, die. This is changing, and thank goodness, because the kind of pressure that has been placed on us to achieve success and money is causing serious social problems. Basically, there is an absence of the message, "it's okay to make mistakes," in Western society.

I believe that everyone can overcome difficulties and come out the other end, even more apt for success. Every time I've overcome a great challenge, I'm stronger, wiser, and I have the ability to be even more successful. I also think more critically. I reject some of the forced societal messaging that's placed on me, and I take calculated risks that have for the most part worked out very well for me. I'm an outlier. There are way few outliers in the world, and we stand out. It's not that I'm actively protesting against societal values. I understand the importance of the values, but guess what? Not every single value that is imposed upon me aligns with my personal values and purpose. If I believed that, I would have been stopped a long time ago from breaking the glass ceiling and winning an election, and from raising a daughter in a stable and loving co-parenting agreement with her father, my ex-husband, with whom I had the most extraordinarily friendly divorce.

Make yourself a promise right now that you will think critically about the values that are imposed on you, particularly when you're up against the wall. Create your own script, because there is no genie in a bottle to grant you 3 wishes. You are your own genie. Get to know yourself, and by the end of this book, I wish for you to discover the beautiful person within that has the strength to do anything they set their own mind to.

Step 2 is about hindsight. The reason I raise being a critical thinker is because you have to look back at what just occurred, analyze it, and make specific modifications for the future. This is true in business and personally. Have you ever watched a person trip as they walk down the sidewalk? What do they do? They look back. They're looking to see what it is they didn't see, or what caused them to trip. Was it a raised piece of concrete, a divot that caught the tip of their shoe? Was it their shoe, and they need to fix it or tie their lace better?

You can immediately see where I'm going with this, right? Step 2 is about looking back and accepting what errors you've made. It's about admitting it, at the very least to yourself, and then atoning, forgiving, and beginning anew. If you've completed Step 1, this will happen a lot more naturally. There are lots of ways to recognize the tiny mistakes in what brought you to this point. When you get quiet with yourself, and take some time for reflection, you may be able to gain some insight on this. As I live in a mountainous region, I've come to a lot of realizations while on hikes. There's something about getting the body moving, and being in nature, that gets me to see that my journey through life is connected to the nature that surrounds me. I can see hope in the rushing waterfalls, which are made more beautiful because of a jutting rock that water finds its way around. I can transform a challenging mountain hike—involving scrambling up rocks and pulling myself up cliffs—into an analogy of life, and it reminds me to view solutions to problems as just a series of small steps that lead to the peak of a mountain.

But, I can admit that I fell into the trap of being a victim too. I was angry that people in my political circle had not supported me as I wanted and needed. In all honesty, there were many who were beyond that; they were vicious. When I was elected, I belonged to this

Step 2 – Putting It Back Together Again

new club that I assumed would guide me and protect me just because we were in the same caucus or cabinet. Now I realize, why should they? To them, this woman just dropped in from out of nowhere and was on their team. They didn't know me at all. For better or worse, I was appointed to Cabinet; and as a minister, especially without any experience in this role, I focused on learning everything I could, as quickly as I could. This meant that while other newly elected MLAs were forming ties with new colleagues, I was in a revolving door of meetings, events, and tours that were scheduled sometimes to the minute. I had never been so exhausted in all my life. When I put "my hindsight is 20/20" rule to this difficult time, I learned that I could have improved the situation by taking the time to foster trusting relationships with my colleagues.

I wanted to be seen as competent, and I was, but I don't think anyone could have known, because I was so busy trying to make as much happen in as short a period as I could. This was a mistake. I not only couldn't appreciate a once in a lifetime experience, but when things got really rough, I was alone. I had few people from my old life; their lives kept going, and I wasn't around. In this new life, I wasn't fully accepted. The expression "out of sight, out of mind" fit. It's not so much that people didn't care, but more that I had lots of superficial connections rather than deep, meaningful relationships. This is something that I work on today because of that experience. I slowly began reaching out to people who have the same values as me, and I understand that it's an investment that grows slowly but on a strong base. I also learned that credibility is established much easier when you establish a good relationship first. People are much kinder and more helpful to people they have a positive rapport with.

My greatest learning from this difficult part of my journey through life has been to "slow down" and "relax." I actually heard this for a long time in many shapes and forms, but I didn't listen. Is there a message that you're being given that you're resisting? There are lots of messages that are transmitted that come in the most interesting forms. Here are a few examples. Do people take advantage of you? Do they make plans and cancel, or not show up or show up late? This may not be the intent they have, but your ego may lead you to believe this. You tell yourself things like, "My time is not valuable to others; they dislike spending time with me; everyone disappoints me; I'm not interesting; I'm not good enough," and the list goes on.

Stop it. You cannot control others and their choices. Often, the real reason is that people are so depressed they don't want to go anywhere; they are overwhelmed and don't keep an organized schedule, and lots of reasons that you will pretty much never fully know. But when you reach out and get silence on the other end, recognize that this is a sign. But it's not about you.

Stand in your own power and treat people with benevolence and understanding. Forgive them, because they probably don't know they've hurt you. And you don't need to tell them either. Let. It. Go. When you see them next time, treat them with kindness and love anyway. This is the natural ebb and flow of life, and if you go around interrupting it by stepping on every stone, you'll never get home. My mother-in-law used to tell me this every time I'd complain about a situation where I felt slighted or my feelings got hurt. I even used to be mad at her for saying it! That's the "relax" message that has been trying to be heard for a long time. I used to want to snub people who hurt me, or "un-friend" them. "I'll show them that I won't be treated that way," I used to believe. I even imagined myself as the perfect person who treated everyone with respect, as I announced angrily, "I would never treat anyone like that!" What BS. Now I recognize that if I had only listened to my mother-in-law's advice, I would have saved myself a lot of tears, sadness, and anger. Over and over, the same message came to me in different ways and, each time, for a long, long time, I put my feigned piety ahead of listening.

Do people tell you not to be so stubborn? The message is to be more open to new ideas. Are you told you're judgemental? The mes-

Step 2 – Putting It Back Together Again

sage is to show more love. Are you accused of being selfish? The message is to give, without expecting reward. Do your friends call you cheap? Stop being envious of others. Have you been called too sensitive? Don't react to everything that is said, as though it is about you. It's not.

Take some time to think about this, because it's very helpful to release these negative perceptions. You will recognize a message because, often, it is the thing that we get offended by. Taking offense comes from a place of denial and insecurity. Even if someone is trying to hurt you, don't get angry, incite revenge, or even call them out. Learn to take joy in peace. You're not perfect, and you never will be; so listen to the messages that are being directed at you, and do your best to be a better person even when others aren't. There is nothing greater than the feeling of release over negative thoughts that shackle you and prevent you from rising up.

The best way to master this is to forgive. First, forgive yourself. Begin by telling yourself that you're doing your best. Your best right now may be getting up and making it to work on time. And if that's the case, be kind to yourself for doing that on a consistent basis. Forgive yourself for not being the perfect child, or the perfect friend, spouse, or colleague. No one else is either. Everyone is just doing what they can. And if you look around and wonder why it seems like they're slacking, I promise there is a reason that you don't know about. So, forgive them.

I truly believe that forgiveness is one of the most powerful tools to recovering from loss and failure. In this process, remember, Step 1 is to get real and move past denial. Step 2 is to take what you've learned from your reality check and make sure you do your best not to trip on that part of the sidewalk again. Use what you learned in hindsight, and forgive yourself for not realizing it at the time, denying it, or plain old having ignored it. And going forward, commit to applying what you've learned.

I truly love how children forgive each other. They are great examples for us to follow. For the most part, when children say sorry, it's immediately forgiven and forgotten, because there's no sense wasting play time on petty feelings. It's not just that their memories aren't as developed. Bad habits and prejudice are taught to children. We all have faulty programming. But that's all it is. We are taught to believe that forgiveness is a sign of weakness. In fact, it takes far more strength to let go of something that you know is an injustice. The greatest thinkers and helpers of our time show this. Nelson Mandela and Victor Frankl, both unjustly imprisoned, were able to articulate how to unlock their freedom through forgiveness. One of the most amazing gestures of forgiveness, to me, is forgiving criminals. I remember reading about the Green River Killer, Gary Leon Ridgway, who admitted he had slayed upwards of 60 female victims. At his sentencing, the families of the victims were able to offer their impact statements. Understandably, there was a lot of anger and rage directed towards him for ruining so many lives. But of all those impact statements, there was only one that penetrated Ridgway's steel exterior. The father of a young teenage girl spoke to Ridgway and told him that the hardest thing he had ever been expected to do was to live up to his faith and forgive. He explained that while so many of the victims' families hated Ridgway, he could not. He ended his statement with a very simple, "You are forgiven sir." It was to these words, that Ridgway was moved to tears. That is the power forgiveness has.

Just like our iPhone regularly gets an upgraded operating system, so is this your opportunity to upgrade to a better, more efficient system that has added features. Forgiveness of yourself, and of others, is like that. It gives you a chance to sweep out old bugs and bad programming that slows you down from reaching success. While you can't upgrade your operating system like a phone, one way to do this is through your own ritual. It's a pretty powerful thing and, when I've done it, I feel a weight lifted.

Step 2 – Putting It Back Together Again

Simply write a letter to those who you want to forgive. Start with yourself. I recommend about a half to ¾ of a page for each person you choose. Praise yourself and others for the good you have seen in them. Include that you know they have their own reasons for treating you poorly, and that you wish them peace and happiness. Be specific about what you are forgiving, and write it as you imagine you would speak to them, if they were standing in front of you. Don't worry about spelling mistakes, or the legibility of your writing. Then take the paper you've written these notes on to a place outdoors where you can safely burn them. Stay and watch the papers burn. Even better is if they can be burned on soil where you can imagine the words being planted like seeds to grow and flourish. Forgiveness is the deepest expression of love. We all deserve to be loved like this. If you would like a template of a letter that you can use for this ritual, it can be found at RenewYourPurposeToday.com, in the Renew Your Purpose workbook.

When you've done the forgiveness ritual, you will begin to feel lighter. Soon, you will notice that your anxiety and worries dissipate and even begin to bother you less and less. Perform this ritual whenever you like. Some people believe in performing this ritual with phases of the moon. It can be a powerful thing to perform this ritual by the light of a full moon. Give it a try!

Another part of moving forward with an understanding of what went wrong in the past, is to find some morning rituals that prepare your mindset for the day. Maybe you suffer from anxiety or depression, and can easily get caught up in negative thoughts even upon waking. Start tomorrow and really take note of what your mind chatters about in the morning when you wake up. Another way of clearing out the unnecessary cobwebs of the past is to use mindfulness. You've likely heard about mindfulness, but let me tell you what it is. Being mindful is the act of taking conscious note of your inner dialogue, your emotions, and senses. You can use mindfulness to set your intentions, by noticing what is going on in a given moment, and then positioning your attitude to accept or modify what you perceive. So, by working through Step 2, you will be able get past your mistakes and current struggles by being mindful of your thoughts.

Let's begin with your thoughts first thing in the morning. When you feel that sense of wakefulness, keep your eyes closed, and first notice all of your senses—the sheets, warm on your skin; the soft fur of your pet curled up nearby—try to only focus on one sensory image at a time. What do you hear? Birds chirping, a car engine, someone shovelling the snow? What smells can you describe? Newly laundered sheets, bacon and eggs, fragrance from a blooming tree? Before you open your eyes, think about two or three things that you're thankful for. Take in a breath slowly through your nostrils, and hold for a few seconds. Let out your breath in a slow exhale. Open your eyes when you're ready to get out of bed, and look around the room, noticing the colours and the brightness level. This short technique is just a small step in the right direction to calming your nervous system each morning so that you can begin your day with more clarity. If you'd like to download this short, mindful morning message, you can find it at RenewYourPurposeToday.com.

Your mind, up to now, if you haven't practiced mindfulness, wanders wherever it wants. If you have anxiety, you may wake and feel a sense of dread, or butterflies in your stomach. This is a sympathetic response to stress. It's the central nervous system acting to prepare the body to flee a harmful situation. Our bodies were built like this to avoid pain, injury, and death. In modern society, all the stress that we are under from external factors, even noise and light pollution is now known to cause the sympathetic nervous system to react. This exercise can help your body recover from stress by sending more oxygen to your brain and cells. Scientific research supports the use of mindfulness to calm the sympathetic response system that is often on overdrive when you perseverate on negative thoughts or have increased levels of stress.

Step 2 – Putting It Back Together Again

Another part of putting your best foot forward, in Step 2, is to create a brand-new slate for yourself.

As you begin to get real with your actions of the past, forgive yourself and others, and change your thought patterns. You may want to consider treating yourself to something new that will create a sense of beginning anew. It doesn't have to be costly or a big change. In fact, it's important to keep it very simple at this stage. It may be something like treating yourself to new, fluffy bath towels, or taking a Saturday to clean your room of old notes in the bedside table, and move around the furniture in your room. Changing your physical space can trick your mind into transitioning to something new. You do similar practices like this, such as getting new clothes or school supplies to begin a new school year. Each new calendar year, you may set resolutions; and to accomplish your goal, you equip yourself with the right tools to motivate you to success. This is the same. It's a personal step forward in the right direction, and so marking it with something special is a way of being kind to yourself, and accepting that it's time to move on from the past.

Some people take more obvious steps to show outwardly that they are changing for the better. A new hairstyle, cut, or colour can also signal to yourself but also to others a fresh attitude. On the other hand, I don't recommend doing anything drastic like getting a tattoo or something permanent or overly dramatic. A tattoo, for example, is a daily reminder that you will see, or at the very least know exists on your body. Do you really want a reminder of this difficult time? In fact, I suggest making only small changes, so that you don't associate anything permanent with this time of your life. You can always move furniture around later or grow out your hair from a short cut. In future steps, you will see the importance of letting go of the past, and how to embrace newfound freedom. It would be a shame to attach a permanent reminder of your current woes. By all means, when you've reached the end of this journey, CELEBRATE! I will absolutely be sharing ideas on how to celebrate, and I hope you'll find some personal joy in doing that.

Now that we've had a good look at how to begin taking your first steps forward after a major setback, let's start thinking about how to build a strong base to create some velocity behind your new movement. So far, we've focused on your inner thoughts and some very personal healing. This is all part of the renewal process. You are slowly replacing old habits, thoughts, and beliefs, with healthy, simple, new ways of seeing yourself as a person who has an important role in the world. Soon, you will begin to notice how your gifts can inspire you, and others around you. And this journey will be something that when you look back, in hindsight, is like a map. In this case, it is the map of your life as you've lived it thus far, and it's full of turns and roadblocks; but it's also full of picturesque moments of gladness that you are in full control to create. The next chapter will show you practical ways to build your strength on this journey to finding your purpose. It's going to be your own antidote formula that will serve you in times ahead.

Chapter 4
Step 3 – The Antidote

"Prevention is better than cure."
– Desiderius Erasmus

4

So, you may have already noticed that I'm not trying to sugar coat your 100 day journey to renew your purpose. And I have good reason for not doing this. If you don't know what the problem truly is, you can't develop solutions that will actually solve the problem. I used to do yearly Occupational Health and Safety (OH&S) training for my teaching staff. It was not only a legal required element of me as a leader each new school year; it was a very effective way to ensure an ounce of prevention kept me from having to deal with a lawsuit. You'd be surprised at the amount of people who try to sue school districts, pretty much to no avail; but nonetheless, I didn't want to be caught off guard with a problem that I hadn't proactively mitigated through training every eye and ear on site.

One of the parts of training involved risk management. I happen to love risk management, and find all sorts of ways to add it to my consulting practice because of what I learned as a school principal. There are just so many ways to safeguard your business, and the same holds true for your own ability to handle your personal crisis. One of the techniques I used in training staff to take on collective accountability for safety was the 5Y technique. It always helped frame the importance of reporting hazards. The 5 Whys technique allows you to look into countermeasures to prevent a problem from recurring. The example I often used was the death caused by shotput. I just made it up, but it got people's attention. Basically, the scenario was that a person's death was caused by a head injury due to a shotput ball being left on the outdoor field of the school. If you don't know what a shotput is, it's a heavy iron ball that is heaved as far as possible in competitive track and field. Back to the 5 Why's - the premise of the exercise is to ask why, 5 times, which will lead to a deeper understanding of the root cause of a problem. In this case, the scenario was set up where, at a school, there was a shotput ball left out on the field; and by Monday morning, the police arrived at the school, wanting to know how the lethal shotput had been left on the field. I'd get the staff to work in pairs or small groups, to ask why, 5 times.

For example:

"Why was there a shotput left on the field?"
– "Because it was missed when the equipment got rounded up."

"Why did it get missed?"
– "Because it was hidden in some tall grass."

"Why was it hidden in the grass?"
– "Because there was a patch that was not maintained."

"Why wasn't it maintained?"
– "Because the caretaker's mower broke down."

"Why did it break down?"
– "The mower is very old and needs to be replaced."

It was a quick activity and I can assure you, teachers are a creative bunch so, the responses often yielded some very funny scenarios to lighten the mood, and always some very specific discussion on not only providing safety, but also other issues that could be present. For example, in this case, if a large piece of equipment needed to be purchased, it could be budgeted or requested from a central budget, etc.

But most importantly, it provided the right type of systems thinking to promote prevention.

That's what this chapter is all about: preparing an antidote to help you learn from your mistakes, but also to help prevent the same event from recurring over again. Read on!

Gratitude...

First of all, for this step, do a check in with yourself. Are you ready to do the work? Have you arrived at some conclusion as to why you are in your current state of mind? Do you have the insight required to make the necessary changes to discover and renew your purpose? Are you taking time to be gentle with yourself and also truthful at the same time? If so, Step 3 is waiting for you, and you'll explore how to start tapping into your purpose by building strength in your physical and emotional state. To do that, I want you to find appreciation for your current situation. WHAT? You want to get as far away from this situation as possible, right? Then you've got to find reasons to appreciate where you're at, as though it was all meant to be. This is a really vital thing to understand, so that you can not only come out the other end whole again, but it's also vital to prevention. We all know about the 2020 pandemic. The world was completely unprepared. Leaders had no experience with this virus that took over world economies and created chaos for citizens in what could be considered the most significant crisis of our time. We learned new ways of coping in business to stay afloat, and some even excelled in this crisis. That is going to be you! By following these steps, you're going to find ways of coping with your situation, and you will be able to apply what you learn, to build a stable future. As you start putting the steps into practice over the next 100 days, you'll see meaningful differences and will feel renewed.

My first suggestion is to begin a regime of thoughtful, meditative practice. I'm not suggesting you get a yoga mat, or even that you find a space that is quiet and reflective, where you can be alone. I know first-hand that this can be a challenge, and if you're like I was in my darkest hours, you're just keeping it together—getting to work on time is a struggle, and you're putting in the minimum to be able to optimize

Step 3 – The Antidote

what little energy you have. So, believe me, I'm not going to ask you to do anything overly taxing, uncomfortable, or inconvenient. Just do this. Commit to spending 10 minutes each day learning to meditate, if you don't know how already; or if you do, choose to indulge yourself in the state of mind stillness that is meditation.

I remember when I began the practice of meditation, I couldn't calm my mind from wandering all over the place. I happened upon a really great app called Headspace. It's taken over the world of meditation apps since then. What I loved, and I really mean LOVED about this app, is that it allowed me to be very forgiving of my initial inability to meditate. It also took me through a series of 10-minute meditations so I could easily learn. I'm all about getting across the finish line one small step at a time, and this app helped me do that.

For me, I found my energy getting zapped by lunch time at work. So, what I did was let my admin assistant know that I would be needing 10 uninterrupted minutes. If you need to tell a white lie to get the time, just do it. It would be preferable to let others in your workplace know that you're taking this time to yourself, but if this doesn't fit in the workplace culture, you've got to put your needs first. Trust me, this small amount of time to yourself, free from sensory overload of people asking you questions while you try eating your lunch, will become GOLDEN time, and you will absolutely be finding more 10-minute segments to add to your antidote repertoire. This is absolutely essential to teaching your central nervous system to remain calm.

The practice of taking in more oxygen, combined with mindfulness and clearing your mind of unnecessary clutter on a regular basis, is no different than working out your muscles. Once it becomes a part of your regular routine, your body will automatically respond; and soon, you begin to feel more in control of your energy, and your thoughts will become clearer. You'll begin to hear the whispers of who you are put on this earth to be. If there is one thing I know, it's that you are here to make a difference. To hear that voice, you have to learn to shut out the clatter, and teach your body and mind that it's safe to be calm. When you reach the calm, your mind and body will start diverting its attention to something other than ringing alarm bells.

Another antidote, which is becoming more and more popular, is something very intriguing. It's called "forest bathing." Doesn't that just conjure up the fragrance of pine, and can't you just hear a gurgling stream, and the sound of your own footsteps on the crisp leaves that have fallen on the ground. Oh yes, forest bathing is extraordinary! It's a Japanese concept called shinrin-yoku, and is established in the belief that being immersed in nature, especially among trees, offers a scientifically proven way to reset our nervous system.

Immersing yourself in the biochemical nectar of trees, in combination with taking in the forest sensorily—the sights, sounds, smells, taste, and touch—is truly an amazing experience. The effects are instantaneous, and you'll be forever seeking ways to achieve the feeling of being in touch with the peace and beauty that nature provides. Its effectiveness has to do with another concept known as "soft fascination." Soft fascination is a part of Attention Restoration Theory as explained by psychologists, Kaplan and Kaplan. There are four states of attention that lead to cognitive restoration, according to Stephen and Rachel Kaplan (1989):

- Clearer head, or concentration
- Mental fatigue recovery
- Soft fascination, or interest
- Reflection and restoration

In the first stage, a clearing of the mind occurs. We began this in Step 2 of this book. In this step, the negative thoughts, concerns, and worries were let go of through the process of getting real and forgiving yourself. You'll note that I didn't ask you to "just get over it." I asked

Step 3 – The Antidote

you to acknowledge the thoughts and feelings; and then, by truly forgiving yourself, the mind and body experienced a natural release, which allowed you to move on to the next step.

In Step 3, similar to the second stage of Attention Restoration Theory (ART), restoration is achieved by learning how to meditate, which is essentially a way of recovering from a state of mental fatigue. Following this, if you add forest bathing to your antidote regime, you will allow yourself to experience the gentle distraction as you engage in this low-stimulation activity. This reduces the internal chatter and clatter, which is needed to optimize your healing and then reach the next and final stage of ART: reflection and restoration.

In this stage, the most significant renewal occurs. You will start to have wonderful moments of lucidity, and your thoughts will start to become more and more organized, allowing you to begin reflecting on your life's goals, and to form logical plans. In the next chapter, which is Step 4, you'll begin the process of reflecting on and prioritizing your desires. But not only that, you'll learn how to put those priorities into action, and what you need to do to stay on track.

In the meantime, while the next step is a really exciting part of the journey, immunizing yourself from repetitive behaviours is essential. So, let's look at the last few parts of creating your best defense from falling backwards. They are: changing the scenery, good nutrition, and resisting distractions.

In Step 3, you are building immunity from the consequences of mistakes: shattered confidence, lack of trust in yourself and others, disappointment, fear, depression, and anxiety, to just point out some. You've established the importance of introducing meditative practices and soft fascination into your regular habits. When you are ready, one way of ensuring you remain committed to the practices in Step 3, is to prepare your space to ensure you have a regular place to practice. I recommend choosing a comfortable place in your home, where you have privacy, or where you can set boundaries with others in your household by letting them know that when you are in your chosen space, you should not be interrupted. I chose my own bedroom and informed others in my home that when I place a small sign on the door, they are not to interrupt. Setting boundaries will be discussed later, but suffice to say for now, in clearing space for your own healing to take place, you will always have a "sanctuary" to restore your cognitive and mental capacity.

Along with setting the stage for your privacy, prepare your space physically. You may want to listen to a meditation from an app on your phone. A link for the app I mentioned earlier, Headspace is on my site RenewYourPurposeToday.com. In that case, it's a good idea to have a set of earphones that stay in your designated space. This will increase your chances of following through, and avoid providing an excuse to not complete your meditation. Adding this familiarity and consistency to your space, also provides a setting that reduces stress and anxiety. You may also like to add other items to the space, like candles, essential oils or an atomizer, a soft and comfortable blanket, or a blue tooth speaker if you prefer to be surrounded by sound. Set your timer and do your best to stick to the time you've given yourself; you deserve it.

On the other hand, you may find yourself falling asleep during these meditation or relaxation sessions. If that's the case, don't be hard on yourself! Your body will react the way it needs to, and if you naturally fall asleep, it's a strong indication of the level of exhaustion that you are actually experiencing. While I'm outlining steps for you to get to a place where you can renew your purpose, this is a good time to tell you that there is absolutely no prescribed timeline. I don't actually use 100 days as a hard and fast rule. You will heal and grow at your own pace based on when you are ready and how disciplined you are. But, it is possible to use time as a measurement for your own goals and also if you are working with my as a client in my 100 day executive consulting program.

Step 3 – The Antidote

What I can tell you is that if you are ready to truly commit to doing the work, you will achieve miraculous growth. But your body will tell you the truth. Sleep is one significant indicator of health. If you can't fall asleep, or find yourself exhausted all the time, it may very well be that there are medical factors such as depression, hormonal imbalance, or other health issues that can only be resolved by working with your doctor. These steps are not about climbing up as fast as you can! You will see in later chapters that this is a program that can always be revisited as a way to reframe and renew your commitment to finding your purpose. The steps don't have to be in order for you to achieve renewal. Sometimes you may have to go back to a previous step, and this is okay (more on this later).

Step 3 also encourages you to look at your nutrition. Your diet is tied to your emotional state and your mental and physical health. I'm including this in Step 3 because I learned by taking the long route that it matters—a lot.

As I mentioned in an earlier chapter, car accidents have been disrupting my life in a very intrusive way! I've had several, and the last one really took a toll on me by causing a serious concussion. I spent the better part of 8 months with chronic migraines; my whole body was tied in knots, I had major brain fog, and was totally exhausted. A friend of mine encouraged me to try a keto diet. Keto is a high fat, low carb regime. There is a lot of information on the internet, and most physicians are knowledgeable about it as well; so suffice to say, I will share my experience since starting keto, and I will leave the research up to you!

I started my keto journey and began counting my carbohydrate intake. It was a major transition to think about the sugar and carbohydrate count in my daily foods. There is sugar in seemingly everything! I started to realize that I'd been consuming massive amounts of sugar, and when my body went into ketosis, which is the state in which your body uses fat for energy instead of carbohydrates, the difference was nothing short of miraculous. Not only did I lose the unwanted weight I had previously put on, I started noticing that the brain fog lifted within a month, the headaches dissipated, and my soft tissue injuries began to improve more rapidly than ever. My memory began to improve, and my mood shifted completely as well! I now have massive—and I do mean massive—amounts of energy that I haven't experienced in many years! In fact, it's a big factor in being able to write this book while working full time, raising a family, and having a whole lot of other responsibilities.

I started getting even more out of my meditation practices, had more energy to get out in nature to reflect, and started returning to the strong confident voice that I hadn't heard for a while. My purpose was starting to emerge!

I've incorporated a number of daily practices and routines, which I will share in later steps. These are now parts of my everyday life, and I don't feel complete without them. By changing my dietary intake, I've opened up a major pathway to my emotional growth. The change in my body makes me feel more confident in how I move, and how I feel about myself. It caused a major breakthrough, returning to physical fitness, and loving it again rather than resisting and eventually abandoning all efforts.

Cognitively, I believe keto has offered me a sharpness and a focus that when combined with my renewed energy, makes me feel unstoppable. Having the ability, capacity, and strength to complete anything I now set my mind to, is the greatest motivator to continue avoiding sugar, and to stay on course with my keto lifestyle. I love how my mood is clear and stable, and my anxiety is manageable without a prescription. My relationships are even improved, because I'm more attentive, more patient, and overall just a happier person. It's a major commitment, but it's one that without which I would not have completed my own journey to renewing my purpose!

Step 3 – The Antidote

Now that you've started to include some important practices to protect you from future setbacks, there's one last part to preparing the best antidote possible. This is, for most, a major challenge. It is the act of avoiding distractions that keep you from achieving your discovery of purpose.

This is a serious topic. There are distractions all around you; some that you are aware of, and others that you use as excuses for NOT committing to completing this journey. Of all the causes of failure to renew your purpose, succumbing to distractions is at the top of the list.

Some distractions are:

- Food
- Alcohol
- Drugs
- Sex
- Electronics
- Shopping
- Gambling

If you are struggling with any of these behavioural or chemical addictions, help is available. Your physician is the first person you should refer to in these circumstances.

We are living in a society with ever-present options to help us avoid our pain. Avoidance is not overcoming. None of these distractions will improve your situation, or be the bullet that unlocks your potential. As you may already have experienced, they are moments that fulfill a quickly fleeting sense of gratification. When the "hit" is over, you need more and more to achieve the levels of gratification that you initially experienced.

The damage to ourselves and our loved ones, caused by addictions, is not unsurmountable. Indeed, you may have even chosen this book because you've been able to overcome your dependence on certain behaviours or substances. If so, you have my complete respect for making it through one of the most difficult challenges that humans face.

If you are just beginning your journey away from addiction or distraction, your best source of help is your medical doctor, who can refer you to the proper resources and professional help.

Should you be fortunate enough to live a life that is addiction and distraction free, appreciate the position you are in. Be mindful of these distractions, and if you find yourself falling prey to the attraction of avoidance, call yourself on it. When you start having that glass of wine every night instead of just on the weekends, or when that glass of wine becomes two, three, or a whole bottle, you will be taking steps backwards. Lean into this as a potential and powerful sign of something you don't want to face. Go within yourself, go back to the practices of this step, and reflect inwardly to try and decipher what it is that you need to acknowledge. If that doesn't jar the message you need to hear, return to Step 1 or 2, and get real with yourself, get help, and forgive yourself for straying from your commitments and following the longer path. Above all, don't worry, because you can always get back on track and, always, be just a bit wiser.

Chapter 5
Step 4 – Version 2.0

"Headlines, in a way, are what mislead you, because bad news is a headline, and gradual improvement is not."
– Bill Gates

5

Step 4 is an exciting new beginning. Let's compare it to the feeling of a brand-new year. So many people look forward to the closing of the calendar year as a way of ending old patterns that didn't serve them, or as a motivator to begin anew on January 1. A New Year's resolution gets you excited about the possibility of new-found happiness. What causes this surge of motivation among the masses? Why do you follow the hype? How do people sustain their motivation to stick to a resolution? What causes you to lose interest and eventually let go of the possibility of completing it? A New Year's resolution is just one example of how our brain responds to the possibility of happiness. Let's explore the idea of using the physiology of our brain to create the perfect setup to unlock the real *meaning* of this book: living a happy life that is fulfilled by YOU. In other words, you are going to learn why external factors like a romantic relationship, food, sex, drugs, or alcohol cannot provide sustainable happiness in your life. However, there is a physiology that can be tapped into, which will put you in the driver's seat to getting what you want and experiencing very deep levels of peace and happiness in your life.

Let's talk about the not-so-secret neurotransmitter, dopamine. First off, you may not know what a neurotransmitter is. If not, the simple definition is that a neurotransmitter is a chemical that acts like a messenger in your nervous system. I explained to you earlier that calming the central nervous system is required before being able to overcome your challenges. The scientific reason behind this is centrally focused on dopamine. There are at least 200 known neurotransmitters in the human neural system, and dopamine is just one of these; but it

Step 4 – Version 2.0

is a very important neurotransmitter to our sense of contentment or pleasure. More importantly, it is also scientifically connected to motivation. The neural system, as you can see, is vital to our emotional and mental health. Knowing how to make this work for you, from a physical, scientific perspective, will accomplish two key elements to overcoming and proactively preparing you for painful moments; it dispels any myth that a person can just "get over it," because you cannot dispute the neurological science of mental health, and understanding how to stimulate dopamine will be a powerful asset to boost you into action.

You can look at the neural system as a circuit in your brain that produces a feeling we like. I'm going to share a reverse example of misusing dopamine, to illustrate the concept you need to master. You're hungry, so your brain is going to send a signal that will cause digestive juices to flow and sugar levels to drop; you might even start to feel this physically. When you eat, dopamine is produced, and your brain recognizes this as satisfaction. Your body feels strong again, and your mind functions better after a healthy meal. Sometimes, especially if you're feeling stressed, you might associate the dopamine fix from eating as comfort. We've all done this. That's why, when your friends show up with a pint of ice cream to indulge in after a break up, it seems like a good alternative to feeling sad. Think about the strong image that is used around food for marketing purposes. There is a very good reason for this: It works. You see, not only is dopamine released after that pint of your favourite peanut butter, chocolate ice cream (Haagen-Dazs for me, thanks!), research has shown that dopamine is transmitted by the mere THOUGHT of this indulgence. Now that's powerful. And that is something that you can use to *meaningfully* transform into motivation!

As I shared with you in the previous steps, getting real with yourself, learning to forgive, and adopting healthy strategies to calm your nervous system are all ways to prepare a strong base for Step 4. And Step 4 is going to completely alter your life. It is the most significant part of your journey to renewing your purpose. It's the working plan to move you towards achieving what you deserve.

So, let's learn some practical ways to add to the strategies you've already practiced. This practical advice is going to set your physical body up for success and, in turn, boost the neurotransmitter *dopamine* into action. You see, if dopamine can be created by the thought of ice cream, damn straight you can also create it with thoughts of envisioning your own dreams.

Here are some ways to increase the levels of dopamine, and a short explanation of why:

Get in Some Cardio Exercise!

This is the most common and most practical advice. When you raise your heart rate and oxygen levels during physical activity, the brain releases some of our favourite neurotransmitters that maintain our mental health, including serotonin and dopamine. All you need is a moderate level of intensity to feel the effects. I recommend setting a goal of 20 minutes per day, doing any form of physical activity that suits you—biking, walking, swimming, running—whatever floats your boat! (The 20-20-20 activation hour I suggest later, will take this into account.)

Eat Foods Rich in Tyrosine

Allow me to introduce you to dopamine's buddy, the amino acid *tyrosine*. Tyrosine can be found in some of the foods listed below, and is dopamine's sidekick because it is dopamine's building block:

- Bananas
- Avocados
- Meat
- Dairy

Step 4 – Version 2.0

- Fish
- Poultry
- Almonds
- Apples
- Leafy green vegetables
- Oatmeal

Listen to Music

Music is a valuable intrinsic power that also stimulates dopamine production. In fact, just as anticipation of eating something delicious triggers the release of dopamine, it is also true of the thought of listening to music. The fact that humans spend trillions each year in the music industry, is just one of many pieces of evidence to support the power of pop or whatever type of music you fancy.

These three powerful ways to increase dopamine production are made even more substantial to your growth when combined with your strategies of meditation, soft fascination. And they will give you a huge boost to proceed with the next aspect of your transformation in Step 4, which is to begin setting some achievable goals.

Make a List of Things You Want to Do This Year

Dopamine loves lists. The very idea of accomplishing something sends dopamine to the rescue! And so, I want you to experience this. Here's what you are going to do!

First, set aside about 20 minutes for yourself to do this exercise. By the way, you'll notice that I use 20 minutes a fair bit when I make suggestions about practices that will help you renew your purpose. This is because 15 minutes is too short of a time mindset, but 20 minutes will eventually push you naturally to a threshold of accepting a half hour of any given practice once you've mastered it, and that will lead to an hour of any good practice after that.

Back to the 20 minutes you are about to take for yourself. It's preferable that you use the Find Your Purpose 2.0 workbook, which can be downloaded for free, at www.findyourpurposetoday.com.

Here's what you'll find in the booklet, and what you'll begin in the next 20 minutes.

Trigger anticipatory success by building off of past success (5 minutes):

Set a timer and take 90 seconds to write down 5 moments of personal glory.

Next, reflect on those moments of great victory and achievement. Who did you believe you were, in those moments? Write a statement that embodies those moments that you can return to. The purpose of the statement is to use it in your daily meditation, and build anticipation by triggering your brain to recall those moments and anticipate new moments that feel the same, similar, and even better! An example of this statement could be, "I am able to achieve my goals because I demonstrate discipline." Or, "I am loved beyond measure, and I love others around me unconditionally."

After recognizing that you have had success in the past by applying certain principles, now your brain will prepare for you to set new goals. Set your timer now for 5 minutes. Within the first minute, repeat your statement above to yourself while also envisioning an image of how you felt in the moments you outlined. Next, create a list of what you want to achieve in the next 5 years. You can brainstorm as many ideas as you like, but make sure they are achievable. The goals should be personal, financial, or career oriented. These are the achievements that will re-capture your moments of glory. (Examples of some of my goals are to travel to Spain with my daughter, pay off my mortgage, establish a healthy workout routine, etc.)

Step 4 – Version 2.0

Now that you have a list of goals, you will already be filled with pleasant thoughts of how relieved you will be to no longer have to pay a monthly mortgage, and what you will be able to use that money for instead. Your brain is already anticipating the feeling! So, the next task is to break down the goals you have, into smaller parcels. By beginning with the end in mind, you will be able to trace a pathway backwards to your starting point.

Next, choose three goals that you want to fulfill in the next year. Beside each of the three goals, explain why this goal has meaning to you.

Now that you have set the stage for the "what" and the "why" of your next 12 months, you can plan even further down the road. What is your timeline for the other goals you want to achieve? Prioritize each of the remaining goals by setting a time to achieve it. Use the chart in your bonus package to fill in your remaining goals of this 5-year plan. For example: Year 3 – Sell my home and buy a retirement home near water.

Let's get granular! Take the set of three goals you have for this year, and commit to what you will do to transform these goals into reality within the next 3 months. You will not only check on these goals quarterly; take one step further and create a weekly check-in! (See #6) Here is what your chart will look like:

Goal	Outcome after 3 months
Travel to Spain with my daughter	Put away $1,500 towards our trip.
Run a 10km race	Work up to running 5km in one stretch.
Start a Ph.D.	Narrow my search to a prospective University.

To continue boosting your anticipation, create a weekly check-in for yourself. It is useful to first choose a regular time in your week to dedicate to this. I choose Sunday mornings, after my morning coffee, and I spend 10 minutes looking back at the last week and re-framing my next steps forward. Print out a copy of each of these charts, and post them somewhere that you will be reminded. Not only will this encourage laser focus, you will also be adding to your dopamine boost when you think of the feeling of accomplishment you'll have when you check these off the list! Here is what your weekly chart could look like:

Week 1	Outcome
Goal 1 Travel to Spain with my daughter	Discuss with Victoria when and where to visit Spain.
Goal 2 Run a 10km race	Run 2km on Monday, Wednesday and Saturday this week.
Goal 3 Start a Ph.D.	Research topics of study and programs available.

This step challenges you to answer the questions of who you are and what you want. The "who" is found in the types of goals you've set for yourself. You've just taken some time to reflect and respond to why these goals will bring meaning to your life. You've also worked through the differentiating factor of who you are NOT, by getting honest with yourself about your life up to this point. These are major game changers.

The response to who you are is found in the rationale behind setting your goals. Go deeper into your reasons behind choosing these goals, by asking the 5 Whys, and you will really begin to have a sense of who you are. Take my goal of travelling to Spain with my daughter, for example. Why do I want to do that? Because we have had some of our best memories while travelling together and experiencing the world. Why do I want to make memories of travelling? Because I want my daughter to have an enriched life of culture, and to learn about other countries and their people. Why do I want her to have this kind of life? Because I want her to have the best life possible, and raise her own children in an environment of rich culture and open mindedness. Why do I want my grandchildren to be raised with enrichment and openness? Because I believe that I have a moral obligation to teach

Step 4 – Version 2.0

them everything I can about this ever-evolving, ever-shrinking world, in order to be as successful as possible. Why do I want my grandchildren to be successful? Because my greatest achievement will be to enjoy a comfortable life where I have a close relationship with family. Why is being comfortable and close to family important? Because this is the centre of my true happiness, and it's what I value most above all else.

So, who I am is someone that appreciates the joy that family can bring. I am also someone who places a great importance on learning. Travel is an excellent way to learn, and I want to have as much flexibility to travel as possible, with those I love. So what I want, besides a close relationship with my family, is also financial abundance. To make these goals come true, I have to manage my fiscal house.

This is a simplified example of deepening your "who" and your "what." It's a great way to keep focused on building towards your dreams, by deepening your purpose. The more you dedicate yourself to expanding this mindset, the more developed and the more enjoyable your pathway towards your goals will become.

I like to take a short amount of time each day to do automatic writing. You guessed it: 20 minutes! In that time, this is the perfect exercise to help guide me to align my goals with my purpose. When you start asking yourself the 5 Whys, if the pathway begins to steer in a direction that is not aligned with the meaning of your goal, you may have strayed into the weeds. That's okay! Give thanks that you are able to re-focus your attention on something else more meaningful. This is an opportunity that is waiting to be taken.

Also, as you begin thinking or writing about the 5 Whys, stay away from using generalities like "we" and "they." Instead of using "we," claim responsibility and use "I," and instead of "they," don't be afraid to ask of others! Say "you."

You are well on your way to executing your plan to discover and renew your purpose now! The instant reward of dopamine that you get from anticipating the fulfillment of your life's dreams, will be working it's *meaning* while you focus on the long-term goal and take care of the short term through your own personal check-ins.

But hey, don't forget to double shot the dopamine boost by treating yourself. Treating yourself doesn't have to be expensive or time consuming either. This is essential to breaking down your pathway to success, into small manageable tasks that are doable and give you instant doses of feeling great because you've accomplished each small step. The greatest part is actually looking back and seeing how each small action accumulates into reaching your milestones and then your ultimate goal! And the success of these steps requires you to acknowledge your achievements, and even those sacrifices, by being kind to yourself.

Here are some great ways to treat yourself:

- Take a little one-on-one with your pet! We've all heard about the health benefits and stress reduction that spending a little time with our furry friends can have. If you don't have a pet, take yourself to the local zoo or pet store to wander around and enjoy.

- Learn something new—maybe a pottery class, a challenging yoga pose, or a new recipe, which can all add to your mindfulness at the same time as offering you some precious "you time."

- Do some mini-redecorating. Choose a room in your home and think about what would make it feel more comfortable. Rearrange the furniture, buy some pillows, or add a convenient side table to enjoy a cup of coffee as you relax in your new space.

- Take yourself on a date. Visit the local museum that you've never been to, or take a long drive out of the city. If you live in a rural area, venture into the city for a coffee in a trendy section of town. Visit a cool pub during Happy Hour, go see a movie, and get to know yourself better.

- Buy yourself a new kitchen gadget. Think about that new mixer you've always wanted, and splurge! If you're on a budget, pick up a set of new wooden spoons or tea towels. There's always yard sales where you can pick up some retro glassware to add some originality to your next martini. And that's like two ways to treat yourself in one—a date and some new stemware!

- Try a new coffee shop. You'll feel good about changing up the same old, same old routine, and maybe you'll discover a new mom and pop café!

- Organize your drawers. I know, I know! You're wondering how this can be a treat to yourself. It may be a chore in a way, but organizing this small space will offer you a feeling of spaciousness and boost your well-being. And hey, you can pay it forward by donating the things you no longer need, to a local charity.

- Make a vision board. You can do this on your own or even with someone else. It's such a wonderful way to focus your powerful thoughts and envision your dreams. You can hang the vision board somewhere special, like above your mirror—or my personal favourite, in the mudroom, where I'll see it as I come and go everyday.

- Cook dinner for someone special. Giving is receiving. Cooking for someone allows them to relax and enjoy. Doing nice things for others, in general, is a great way to deepen the intimacy of your relationships.

- Light candles. This is a simple way to add a soft glow to your space and promote relaxation. Your body will even begin producing melatonin, and you'll find yourself relaxing easily in the soft amber light and soft scents that will have a calming effect.

- Go through old photographs. Indulge yourself with some time to go through some happy times. This is even more fun with a friend or family member, where you can fill in the stories of the past.

- Plan a road trip. Isn't most of the enjoyment of a road trip the planning part? Travel is a great way to add some novelty to your regular routines as well. Exploring is one of the best types of self-care, and it's even better if you add some soft fascination to your trip, with a little forest bathing!

Chapter 6
Step 5 – On Growth and Grief

"It isn't the mountains ahead to climb that wear you out; it's the pebble in your shoe."
— Muhammad Ali

6

I have never wanted to climb Mount Everest. I know people who do and some who have. I even know someone who has summitted Mount Everest twice! That's brave. The discipline involved is nothing short of heroic. I think I'm not attracted to the idea because I've always been in a rush to move on to the next thing. It's something I'm working on, believe me. I no sooner complete one achievement and then look out onto the horizon for something new to tackle. Everest is not something you tackle and move onto the next thing, or you'll die—literally. There are about 200-plus bodies leading to the summit of Mount Everest. Removing a body on this kind of climbing adventure could cost another life. It's just too dangerous. There are many causes of death on the climb to the top of Mount Everest. Many die in avalanches; others succumb to exhaustion or acute mountain sickness. This is the result of the effects of altitude on the body. It's a generally accepted strategic necessity to acclimatize on the trek to the summit. This helps the body adapt to the lack of oxygen at high elevation. To do this, mountaineers say that the trek down is the most important key to summiting Everest. Huh? How do you summit Everest if you're climbing down??

Just like the journey you're on now, the climb is steep and, to get to the top, you sometimes need to go back down to acclimatize. Look at it as just part of the process to get to that summit, because the alternative, as I explained above, is far less attractive than taking the time to acclimatize. Wait until you hear how the acclimatization process works though! You'll have even more respect for climbers, and perhaps more appreciation for the parts of your journey when you

Step 5 – On Growth and Grief

feel like you're going backwards or simply standing still. It's all part of the growth process to making you stronger, so keep this in mind as you read on.

The first part of climbing up the almost 9,000 m trek to Everest's peak, is getting to Base Camp. This is a pretty special little spot to begin the summitting journey. And if you plan to summit Everest, you'll be revisiting it, at least a few times. Get this: To summit Everest, there are 3 camps on the way to the summit. Each time they reach a camp, most climbers will return to base camp, to acclimatize. Their bodies will get stronger as they acclimatize and, with this gained strength, they will do the trek and subsequential return trip to Base Camp, another 3 times in total before actually summitting! The next time you meet someone who has summitted Mount Everest, keep this in mind, because you are speaking to a remarkable human.

The point, of course, is that just like those courageous climbers, you too will find that the mountain you climb to discover your purpose, is sometimes longer than you expected. But great achievements are like that. The benefits of returning to Base Camp are all geared to growth. Climbers begin to digest food better, sleep more soundly, and even have time to think over their climb. Climbing wounds and aches begin to heal more rapidly. Only after a few days, the climber feels incredible growth and increased strength.

So, get your climbing gear packed, and be prepared to have to return to Base Camp along your trek. But this isn't a setback at all. It's a strategy to prepare you to be able to make it, not just to Camp 2 or 3 but all the way to the summit. Remember that the longest journeys, like summiting Everest, require the most courage and yield the highest peaks!

That said, I'd like to return to a few things that you need to watch for. Step 5 is a check-in step, so let's really make sure that you've acclimatized to the current camp before moving on to the last 3 steps, shall we? For all my politician friends who read up to this point, you'll all be nodding in agreement about this next part. I know this because, looking back, I received this advice from politicians before me, who left public life. Some left gracefully; others, and certainly most that I know, found it a great loss. I remember the tailspin I felt once the initial shock of my own loss began to set in. I called up a former politician, who had served before me and that I considered to be a mentor of sorts. Although we didn't serve together, I watched him as a young member of our party, and he always had a strong impression on me. He always seemed extremely positive and helpful, and he encouraged me when I thought of running. So, when I was faced with loss, I felt like he was the kind of person who could offer me some fatherly-like advice, and that, he did.

We met at a downtown coffee shop on a sunny spring day. It was a little too sunny for me, I recall, since I was pretty much hiding under the covers and hoping this terrible feeling would go away. True to my impatient character, I was already wanting to talk about next steps, of course. I didn't know about the Base Camp idea at the time. I can't even completely recall our whole conversation, but I was struck with compassion for him when he shared that losing an election was, for him, like experiencing a death. I had never thought of him in this vulnerable light before. I mean, growing up, he was known as Mr. Colgate because he had this beautiful smile that filled a room. He had that smile every time I saw him, and I never once thought it could ever cover grief. Grief... I was determined to avoid that. I was sure that I was tough enough to just keep trekking. I expected him to share advice on how to get ahead again, but he shared this? I was confounded. I was even a bit sad because it was like realizing that Superman was Clark Kent. He was one of my political heroes. How could he ever have been weakened by grief?

The answer is simple. We all have our own kryptonite, and grief is probably the most common form of it. So, as I said before, get to know grief, because when you can recognize it, you can get yourself to Base

Step 5 – On Growth and Grief

Camp and acclimatize. Here are some interesting physical signs to watch for. And these are also signs that you will spot in others, now that you know what grief looks like. Part of our own healing is through the healing of others. It is after summiting our own painful journey that we can guide others through theirs.

Physical Signs of Intense Grief

- Exhaustion
- Sleeplessness
- Over-sleeping
- Weight gain
- Weight loss
- Breathlessness
- Aches and pains, such as chest pain and headaches
- Shaking and increased heart rate
- Feeling sick
- Upset stomach
- Oversensitivity to noise and light
- Skin problems and sensitivity
- Lower resistance to illness in general
- Driving difficulties

All of these are part of the healing process. Take, for example, breathlessness. I can recall noticing this one day. I was constantly sighing. It's as though you are holding your breath and thinking regretful thoughts all day, every day. I don't even remember when it started to improve. But the impact it has on others around you is why I bring it up in this list. Others will immediately ask you what's wrong or if you're okay. You may even get annoyed by this. I did. Until I noticed that it must be annoying to others! Or they will get uncomfortable and not know what to say. This last one is the most common. So, watch for this in yourself, and recognize that your body is asking you for more oxygen. It fits perfectly with the Base Camp analogy, doesn't it? It's your body telling you to return to Base Camp or, in this case, back to

Step 2 or 3, to revisit some of the practices, like meditation and mindfulness, to recalibrate your physical and emotional centres.

I realize this sounds like Step 5 is a step backwards, but you will absolutely experience this reset step. So, I want you to prepare for it, and be equipped with patience to be able to take the time to acclimatize. I wish I would have accepted this part of my journey and taken some time for healing on the forefront. If I could do it all over again, I would find a local grief support group, rather than have just read Kubler-Ross. Once I read her book, I felt I could check the box. But true to what my political mentor told me, I was indeed in the throes of grief. And of course, I was! I had lost my mother, who was like my best friend, and then was defeated publicly, again shamed in the newspapers for all to see. And it just kept on going like that for years. I lost others who formed my inner circle, to unexpected death—an accident on the highway, caused by a snowstorm, killed a dear friend, and then another was killed in a fluke plane crash. It was not fair. But my faith became stronger, and I began to realize that God was forcing me to slow down and take care of myself. Every time I resisted, something painful would occur to cause me to have to return to Base Camp. I can be a very stubborn woman, so I returned to Base Camp for four years. It was as though I was stripped down to nothing. And from there, I began to recognize myself again.

I was angry with God too. I screamed up to the sky with all my might. It did no good. But I do believe this: No matter the depths of emotional darkness that I was in, I never lost sight of the light, although at times it seemed so dim. That kept me alive. It was my own personal Base Camp and, to me, God kept me comfortable enough that I survived, but He also made me uncomfortable enough that I had to grow. I finally surrendered enough to let the hurt go, but I made my journey longer, more painful, and more chaotic by not respecting the power of grief.

Step 5 – On Growth and Grief

Some losses are traumatic. These can be especially difficult to talk about, or even tell others about. On the other hand, there is so much to be gained by releasing the psychological and physical weight of stored painful memories. Think about it as though you're climbing to that summit. You are better off with less in your pack, for sure. In fact, carrying too heavy a load can prove to be far more destructive.

There is plenty of supportive evidence and research to suggest that grief journaling after a significant loss can have therapeutic value. Some experts explain that reconstructing your personal self-narrative is essential to the healing process. I can see why this is true. I used to pray to have "the dream" others told me about, where their loved one visited them. I longed for that dream every night so I could talk to my mom just for a minute. It never came. I still, to this day, have never had that dream. But I started talking to her aloud and then decided more recently to write to her. It's through this, that miraculous healing has taken place. The emotional connection and physical outlet combined into a cathartic tool for me to find insight and cohesion. You can use a grief journal to express yourself fearlessly, without judgement. And perhaps the most useful is to note recurring patterns and dramatic growth.

Here's how to do it:

Write Fearlessly

- Grief journaling is not about writing perfectly.
- Keep your pen gliding on the page, writing without pausing.
- Don't cross out. Even if you write something you didn't mean, leave it.
- Never mind about spelling, punctuation, or grammar.
- Don't be concerned about staying in the lines or margins! Go for it, and be wild on paper.
- Lose control. Don't think. Don't get logical.

- If something comes up in your writing that is scary or makes you feel vulnerable, dive right into it. It means this is an important emotion to process.

I've turned my grief journal into a regular daily routine. I spend 20 minutes each morning dumping out all my thoughts messily into a notebook. I've evolved into using it as a way of encouraging myself through positive affirmations as well. I will share more on this in the next chapter, as a part of Step 6.

At first, you may like to frame your writing with some "journal writing prompts," in case you get stuck! A "grief journal writing prompt" is like a jumping off sentence. Here are some examples that you can incorporate into your writing:

- I remember when…
- I want to tell you about…
- This is what I have to say to you…
- The first time I…
- My happiest memory of you is…
- The greatest lesson I have learned is…

You can even write your story of loss in the third person. This way of looking at your situation, from the outside inward, can be very helpful in expressing compassion towards yourself as well.

In the next step, you'll incorporate your journal writing into some very easy but highly useful tools, to begin tapping into and renewing your purpose. Your purpose is beginning to be set free! For now, try out your journal writing talent here, and see how enjoyable and insightfully stimulating it is! Or visit RenewYourPurposeToday.com to download a journal that I've designed just for you.

Step 5 – On Growth and Grief

Get yourself started here:

Date:

Journal Prompt of the day...

This makes me think of...

www.RenewYourPurposeToday.com

Date:
Journal prompt of the day...
This makes me think of...
Doodle away!

Chapter 7
Step 6 – Make Your Bed!

"If you can't do the little things right, you will never do the big things right."
– William H. McRaven

www.RenewYourPurposeToday.com

7

There's actually a book written by a Navy Seal, William H. McRaven, called *Make Your Bed: Little Things That Can Change Your Life...and Maybe the World*. I've never read it, but it's based on an inspiring graduation speech he gave, which begins with this true statement.

"If you want to change the world, start off by making your bed... If you make your bed every morning, you will have accomplished the first task of the day. It will give you a small sense of pride...."

You know, this guy is right. I never used to make my bed. I mean, never. To be honest, it's kind of embarrassing to admit. But I used to think, why make a neat and tidy bed when I'm just going to mess it up again?

Not anymore. There are now a few non-negotiables that are part of my every day, and making my bed is the first one. Now, I would not have been motivated by this concept a few years back, since basically, I didn't want to even leave my bed some days. I mean, the struggle was real. At some point, the steps that I've begun outlining for you, began to take serious shape in my life; and one day, I decided to treat myself with a new duvet. The first day I woke up in the new fluffy duvet, it was so soft and luxurious that I decided I should make my bed. And I liked the idea of tucking in the sheets at the corners, lining up the duvet evenly, and placing all the pillows in a nice stack. It made me feel like I had accomplished something just for me. And just like the Navy Seal says, it's the first task of the day. Check, done! And

Step 6 – Make Your Bed!

that's not all. Making my bed also made me appreciate the privacy and solace I have in my room. I cleared away all the clutter, and it feels like a space of clarity for me. My sleep has even improved since clearing away unnecessary objects.

Now, making my bed is the first thing I do, and it makes me feel like the day is waiting for me. It's just a mindset change, and so simple. It's easily done because it only takes a minute, or two if you really want to get technical about making the hospital corners. And so I realized that my next step to feeling great, and putting the right foot forward so that I could focus on what's important, was about creating touchstone simple routines that improve my mindset to begin each day.

Step 6 is "Make Your Bed!" But Step 6 also involves a few other important tasks of each day. I realize why these things mean so much. They provide comfort and stability to each day. The simple routines that I've developed are the things in my day that I take complete control of, and even though they are small things, I know they will be a part of each day. I can't even get through a day without stopping to complete these tasks. This means that I've put my own needs ahead of other less important tasks and behaviours. I even say no to anything that interferes with accomplishing these tasks. And when you say no to others, you are saying yes to yourself. This is about building self-respect and boundaries. It's about taking care of yourself and prioritizing your needs, so that your emotional and physical cups are full, or at least being replenished regularly.

What is more, when you start saying no to things that "dis"tract you from your simple goals, you begin to "at"tract people, events, and opportunities that align with your purpose. To all the women out there, pay special attention to this, because we were mostly raised to believe that we must say yes when others ask. The very concept and mindset of saying no to distractions, places you squarely in the driver's seat. You and your purpose become front and centre. Here is an example:

I dated a guy a few times, and I kept noticing some red flags. He was kind of flakey. We would begin a text conversation about going out, and it would get left in the middle of nowhere. Or we would make plans, and ultimately he would ask for a rain check. Well, this didn't work for me, because I absolutely guard my time, and I felt like he showed disrespect of my schedule. And let's be very honest, that's exactly what he was doing. He gave me a lame excuse one time, after asking if it was okay to postpone going on a short trail walk. This was his excuse: His sons would be staying an additional day with him, and so could we please reschedule. Okay, you're saying, but it's his kids! Here's the thing. He has two grown sons—adults who move between his place and his ex-wife's. They probably were not going to be disrupted by his taking a couple hours to do a short trail walk.

He made the commitment, and I looked forward to catching up with him, getting outdoors, and checking out a new trail, in the city, which I hadn't been to. I put the time in my schedule. It was locked in—no wishy-washy changing of plans and moving things to another day because something better comes along. He simply chose to spend the time how it suited him, although he committed to spending the time going on a walk with me. That's disrespectful of my time. Now, I didn't bother putting this out there to him, because this is my value and obviously not his. I simply said that I understood, and for him to enjoy his time. And I meant it. This is key. You can't say things and not mean them, because it doesn't have the same impact on your mindset.

And this is why I meant it. I was actually affronted by his "could give a damn" attitude about me and my schedule, but telling him would not amount to anything. I simply sorted through my mindset quietly and asked myself a few "why" questions. And I realized, as I mentioned earlier, I took offense because he hit on something I value intensely: giving my time to others, and also when others give their time to me. It's clear that we have a centrally important misalignment, and that I'm seeing this as a very clear message—he doesn't follow

Step 6 – *Make Your Bed!*

through on words, he renegotiates commitments, contacts me when it suits him, and expects me to put his need to maintain flexibility in case something more important comes up—*crystal clear*. When I told him I understood, I was telling the truth. I absolutely understood this: My time is valuable, and so am I. I choose people to be part of my life who demonstrate this same value.

But he still got what he wanted, and you are left without anything to do, you say? Wrong. I found gratitude in his action by understanding that he is not someone that I want in my inner circle, because I seek harmony. When I said I understood, I also committed to myself that I would never make plans with him again. I won't be mean or sarcastic, or ever tell him directly that he affronted me. I will simply, over time, not accept his invitations; and, eventually, the space that he took up in my circle of influence will be replaced. And guess what else? That space is absolutely going to be filled with someone who appreciates the time that I give to them, and who I will equally show appreciation for the time they have shared with me.

Do this for yourself. You will start to see that people who bring nothing positive to your growth, and don't inspire you, will begin to diminish in numbers. But more importantly, slowly, you will attract those who demonstrate the qualities that you accept. So, get clear about the core values you possess, and gently and respectfully communicate that to others. They will begin to change their behaviour towards you, or be pruned off your friendship tree. And as is the case with trees, the blossoms become more plentiful and the branches strengthen. This will help you stay committed to your simple routines, and the big plans will begin to also materialize when this is in order.

And back to routines that put you in a mindset for success each day. There is something golden that I want to share with you. I began doing this to start my day on a strong and positive foot. Let me preface it by saying that when you're ready to begin Step 6, your body will let you know. It will be to no avail to begin this step before you're absolutely ready. A good indicator of being ready is the making of your bed upon waking every day. If your physical and emotional harmony are synced, you are ready to start this next, very basic but illuminating exercise!

The reason all should be in order ahead of time is because you are about to give yourself time. Time is, in my opinion, the greatest gift. You've already read about how much I value time, and there is a very simple reason for this. It is the only thing that we cannot make more of. We can't recycle, upcycle, or reuse it. When it's given, it cannot be taken back. No one is inventing more time.

Just think about the one thing that people so often wish they could have more of. Especially when it's scarce. I may have come to this conclusion when my mother was diagnosed with cancer. When she told me, it was over the phone, as we were in different cities. I literally felt my heart break. I wanted to be right there next to her in that moment. Luckily, my superintendent, at work, understood the value of time. He gave me one of the greatest gifts anyone has ever given me. That was the gift of as much time as I needed, to be with my mother through her treatment. I can never fully articulate my gratitude to him for that. It allowed me to be with her when she needed me most. Our relationship grew because of this, and all the little things mattered. I have the most beautiful memories of the time spent with my mother, because it was marked time, I knew it was scarce, and it was worth more than anything I could materially possess. Now that she is gone, those moments have even more value.

I have figured out a way to create more time. Well, not exactly, but like *meaning*, in general, using the combination of belief and perception, I create more time for myself each day. Here's how.

I give myself three 20-minute gifts of time every day. Ideally, you take this time before the rest of the world is up. I'm not a morning person, believe me. But since I've rolled back my clock to start my day

Step 6 – Make Your Bed!

an hour earlier each day, my days begin with a powerful edge that allows me to conquer challenges and fully appreciate the opportunities.

Here's how it works:

After I make my bed, I put on my comfy housecoat and head to my favourite spot overlooking my yard—with my coffee, notebook, and favourite pen. I do have a thing about pens. It must be black ink, and fine-tipped. When I've set my space with the appropriate accoutrements just mentioned, I also set a timer, for 20 minutes. I softly engage my senses to what is around me—the sunlight peeking through the roof tops, the flutter of chirping birds, my cat purring. Pen to paper, I write. I also sometimes doodle and express whatever I want on paper. This time, and these words, are just for me. I don't go back to read what I've written, because it's my way of processing things that have passed. When you do this practice, you will get some really great ideas, and you may want to circle those, take a photo, or whatever works, if you feel the need to transfer them to your work or personal life. But it's meant to be an extension of processing emotions, thoughts, and random distractions that occupy space in your mind. Similar to dreaming, it's a very random process, but since you're awake and actively writing, you can approach it with a spirit of freedom and release, like your brain naturally does as you sleep. Don't be concerned if seemingly irrelevant, odd, or even scary thoughts run out of your pen. This is okay. No one is going to read it or judge it.

The release on paper, first thing in the day, can help you get out any anxiety that you may be holding, which is helpful in organizing your thoughts. If you're facing something mission critical in your day, writing it out through this type of automaticity, will help you articulate the chain of actions that you need to perform. It brings clarity to your actions, and when you receive clarity on paper, through visual and kinesthetic means of writing, you'll find yourself in lucid thought about the order of your actions unfolding, as you set about other behaviours, like walking or driving to work. Sometimes you'll have seemingly little or nothing to write on the paper. If this is the case, I suggest writing various positive affirmations, such as, "I see examples of care and hope all around me." You may also come up with blank statements, such as, "This morning, I write in my journal," and repeat this sentence over and over until some other thought moves in; and you can pick up your automatic writing with this new thought. The idea is to coordinate the movement of your pen with your free thoughts. Doing this will help you release cognitively, and free emotions that may be hidden subconsciously or even repressed.

I've gotten a lot of "aha" moments during this process, but also afterwards, as I proceed to other regular daily tasks. You can see how including this in my daily gift of time has helped me define my own purpose. Throughout the last few years, I've used the ideas and thoughts that arise in my daily gift of time, to make big advances for my own business, like figuring out my niche as an executive consultant working specifically with women leaders. It's like a supply chain, lining up actions that need to occur in an optimized sequence to get results or save costs. Like *meaning*, I realized that this is the greatest strength that I bring to my clients. It's my superpower. Being able to abstractly envision a chain of events comes naturally to me, but when I combine it with this kind of random free thinking, I've experienced moments where I can unlock the weak link and am able to redesign entire service provision chains that have helped many organizations optimize their operations, to expand, and increase profits. Since this is my bread and butter, I need to take special care of this superpower, which for me is part of what forms my own purpose.

This leads to the next 20-minute gift you can give yourself: optimizing your heart rate.

You may be surprised that it doesn't take being a marathon runner to reach your optimal heart rate, and achieve the physical and psychological benefits of physical fitness. This means that physical fitness is available to everyone. It is always best to check with your family

Step 6 – Make Your Bed!

physician about a health program that is right for you.

This is just one way of thinking about your physical fitness, and it can help your mindset about getting physical.

Back to the gift of time, you can see that 20 minutes is my favourite time slot! That's because 15 minutes is doable for any activity, but 20 minutes adds a little boost of challenge that will make you feel accomplished. After my 20 minutes of writing, I head to my stationary bike. It's actually my hybrid bike that I set up on a stationary bike pedestal, which I bought for $30 off Kijiji. I hop on my bike for 20 minutes, and using my Fitbit that I bought for $126 at London Drugs, I check it for my optimal or target heart rate zone. It's not hard to do this, and by the time I reach the 15-minute mark, I'm 75% through my daily workout. This, added to my keto regime, has improved my cardiovascular fitness, motivated me to engage in other forms of fitness, like hiking and snowshoeing, and I'm even setting a small goal to return to long distance running and complete a 10 km race. (I used to be a marathoner, so back to small steps, folks; it's okay to go back to the beginning, remember!) Also, I feel like a morning warrior when I hop off that bike! The endorphins and dopamine are flooding my body before I even step into my first meeting or task of the day. That's an amazing feeling, which you will have!

Have a look at this chart to find your optimal target heart rate zone, and start slowly incorporating this time gift into your day. You'll be glad you did.

These figures are based on the average target heart rate zone for certain ages. You can use these as a general guide.

Age	Target HR Zone 50-85%	Average Maximum Heart Rate, 100%
20 years	100-170 beats per minute (bpm)	200 bpm
30 years	95-162 bpm	190 bpm
35 years	93-157 bpm	185 bpm
40 years	90-153 bpm	180 bpm
45 years	88-149 bpm	175 bpm
50 years	85-145 bpm	170 bpm
55 years	83-140 bpm	165 bpm
60 years	80-136 bpm	160 bpm
65 years	78-132 bpm	155 bpm
70 years	75-128 bpm	150 bpm

There's one last gift you can add to your daily gift of time: learn something new! Along with my own 20 minutes of free writing, and 20 minutes of physical activity, I also give myself 20 minutes each day to learn something new. This makes a full hour of time to give to yourself every day! I sometimes incorporate this part with my physical activity, which I highly recommend. You know exactly what to do here! That's right; put on a podcast, watch a YouTube video, or listen to an audio book. It's such a treat. No more excuses that you don't have time to learn how to create that backyard pond! You can YouTube it and watch how it's done. That's how I now have a perfect little oasis in my own backyard, which I designed, dug, and built (with a little help from my daughter, her dad, and my favourite nephew!).

Can you see how this very small commitment, to giving yourself the gift of time, allows you to zero in on your purpose? The unconscious mind knows what you love. It will tell you by bringing to the surface the messages that are meant just for you, if you let it. This is an imperative to discovering your purpose.

Step 6 – Make Your Bed!

Try it for a week. You have nothing to lose. And if you think this is a great way to get you moving in the right direction, you'll love the next chapter, which is about strengthening your daily routines and the practices you've adopted from previous steps. You're about to become BULLET PROOF!

Chapter 8
Step 7 – Becoming Bullet Proof

"The happiness of your life depends upon the quality of your thoughts; therefore, guard accordingly, and take care that you entertain no notions unsuitable to virtue and reasonable nature."
— Marcus Aurelius

8

I have to tell you something. It's about positive affirmations. You see, they don't actually work. At least according to some of the current research that's out there. I've read up on this because I have often used positive affirmations as a tool for myself, as well as for my clients. So imagine my surprise, and profound disappointment, to learn that they don't work! But I learned something else that is to my great relief. Positive affirmations can be helpful if you are already in a state of mind to accept them as truthful. That means that positive affirmations can be helpful when you're getting ready to be geared up for a presentation that you feel good about, or running that race that you've trained months for.

The latest research shows that when a person is feeling low, depressed, or is going through a tumultuous time, positive affirmations can reinforce the negative feeling they are carrying about themselves, their behaviour, performance, and perceptions in general.

When a person is trying to escape negative thinking, or has low self-esteem, positive affirmations can actually make them feel more hopeless about their situation. So, that news has changed my own view on affirmations. They are better combined with a solid base of high performance that has been built. This is the base you are pursuing by reading and taking action through this book. Positive affirmations can be great tools to use with athletes and high performers who need to remain focused. But in the case where you've fallen from grace, positive affirmations will offer little value to increase a person's motivation or self-esteem.

Step 7 – Becoming Bullet Proof

I do have a challenge to such research. Negative perception of self is often created by reinforcement of negative self-talk or consistent verbal abuse. I believe that while positive affirmations are not the panacea to overcoming low self-esteem, they can provide statements of hope when offered as a show of belief in someone. After all, this is what resiliency building is based on. Resiliency building occurs when you tune into your adaptive skills, and are also reinforced by others that you trust, to apply those skills to practical life. So, even though there is merit to not forcing positive affirmations on an individual who is in the throes of healing, rather than in thriving mode, let's not toss the baby out with the bath water here!

Well crafted, positive affirmations can provide comfort and hope, even if they can't change a person's perception of self. For example, a statement like "I rest my mind and body to improve my health," is more helpful than, "My mind and body are healthy." One implies that there is a pathway to health by resting, whereas the other may in fact be completely inaccurate. Our minds can be tricked, but when we know something to be false, our minds will reject it, and this is why positive affirmations don't work. We are not in a state of mind to truly believe them.

Try crafting a few statements for yourself that will help you in times where you need comfort, rather than when you are revved up for action. Here are a few to start you out:

- I am thankful for what I have, and show gratitude for small graces, as well as for great miracles.

- I can choose to still my mind and find peace.

- All around me, there are examples of love and caring.

- My world, though imperfect, is evolving, and tomorrow I can begin anew.

These affirmations will work best if you've done the work in the first 6 Steps. The power in using affirmations, in making yourself bulletproof, is contingent upon the strength of the base you've built up to this point. Using positive affirmations can help keep you up when you get up, and to begin seeing your world from a constructive point of view, if you have built a robust self-esteem.

This brings us to challenging something else we've been socialized to do: surrounding yourself with positive people. These days, that is sometimes called "toxic positivity." Actually surrounding yourself with people that are always positive, can have the opposite effect. Interesting, right? Think about this for a moment. People that are always positive, when you're down, are actually annoying—sometimes telling you that you should just shake it off, move on, and then adding how amazing their life currently is. I've never understood why some people behave like this. It seems almost cruel. I've pondered that maybe these types are insecure and need to validate themselves by bragging or turning the conversation back to themselves. Maybe they are uncomfortable with emotions that are not exceedingly positive. I can tell you that when I'm at my worst, I don't appreciate being around friends that can't handle the reality of life, which is sometimes pretty ugly.

People who are chronically positive are not trying to make you feel worse, but when they change the topic abruptly from your disclosure that you're having a really challenging day, and quip a response, like "look at the bright side," what they actually do is make you feel worse. This is what toxic positivity does. It excludes people from the conversation, who can't relate to finding the bright side in that moment. We can all improve our level of sophistication on decreasing toxic positivity, frankly. And let's be really honest about the positively toxics that are out there. They don't feel comfortable hearing your truth, because they don't know if they can help. Or some may be in the depths of their own crisis, and they don't have the emotional capacity to help anyway. But nonetheless, I want you to be aware of toxic positivity so that we can all do a little bit better in a world that

Step 7 – Becoming Bullet Proof

needs more comfort, and have less shutting down of people for not measuring up to the positivity meter. So, here are some examples of what toxic positivity looks like, and ways to reframe statements that cause people to shut down rather than speak up. If you can raise the bar of discourse on this topic, you will begin to think in a whole new way, and this will show up in how you treat others. It's about showing compassion and empathy. In the end, after all, how we treat others really does come back to us.

Toxic positivity is...

- Feeling guilty, or like you're a bad person for having negative feelings.
- When others invalidate your true feelings, with feel-good statements.
- When you repress or stuff your emotions and try to move on.
- When you mask your emotions "with a smile."

Here are some ways to alter the toxicity into bulletproof statements that comfort and validate yourself and others...

- Instead of...Only cool vibes allowed. Try... All vibes are welcome here.
- Instead of...Just get over it! Try...I know this seems really hard right now, but don't forget that you've done hard things before, and I believe in you
- Instead of...Think happy thoughts! Try... It's probably really hard to feel positivity right now, but I'm putting out good energy into the universe/I'm praying for you...
- Instead of...Look at the good in everything! Try... It's difficult to make sense of this situation, but in time, we'll sort it out
- Instead of...Don't be so negative! Try... It is normal to have some negativity in this circumstance.

At the end of the day, we are all going to be in the type of situation that will require someone to help us out. Just like a Kevlar vest is meant to protect vital organs, no one is actually completely bulletproof. If you've ever seen a Kevlar vest (bulletproof vest), it covers the chest area and upper body, but not the head. So, if we use this analogy to protect your own thoughts, you realize the importance of bulletproofing your head. By this, I mean bulletproofing your mind, by accepting positive affirmations without the toxicity, and also being better at validating yourself and others when negative thoughts do occur.

Validating others is also a good way to keep your ego in check. There's nothing nice about the friend who likes to brag or flaunt things in front of someone who is going through a difficult time. I believe that karma comes back around to roost, when you forget that we all crawled before we could walk. The expression, "You meet the same people on the way down the ladder as you met on the way up," rings very true here. And when you have been selfish or judgmental, there will be an atonement that you'll have to face.

So, speaking of bulletproofing yourself, if you don't want to be staring down the barrel of someone else's revenge directed at you, it's best to remember that memories are long, and that karma has really good aim.

This is, for me, why slowing down has been such an important part of renewing my purpose. I can think of plenty of examples where my need to get everything done just right, and in record time, caused me to forget to thank people that got me to the next level. Worse are the times I can remember being overly critical, and even extremely harsh on people who made mistakes. I cut them out of my life, or hurt them so deeply that they left on their own. All for what? So that I could get to where I thought I was going. I have two examples to drive this point home. The first one is keeping a tidy bathroom. It's the little things, like taking the time to put the cap on the toothpaste, or putting back the nail clippers where you found them. Slowing down and not behaving like you're some superhero that needs to fly to the tallest building in a single bound, will prevent you from making big messes. It will also save you time in the long run, when those nail clippers are exactly where you took the time to put them.

The second example is more likely to change your perspective about taking the time to keep your ego in check, and treating people with care and respect. It's a regret about a time I did not take less than 15 minutes to do something for my mom. It was washing her dishes. It was a regular crazy end of a Thursday, and I was heading to Calgary from the Legislature in Edmonton, to make a 7:30 p.m. meeting with my constituency association. It's a 3-hour drive from Edmonton to Calgary, and I stopped by to see my mom, who was feeling progressively more and more ill. Her cancer was spreading, but she kept from me how truly bad she must have been feeling.

When I arrived to see her, she had dishes in the sink. This was unusual. She always took care of this kind of chore. I could tell that the dishes had piled up over a couple of days. Again, this was unlike her. I arrived in a flurry at about 4 p.m., and told her I had to get on the highway right away. I really wanted to sit with her and just listen to how she was doing. I saw the dishes, and I offered to wash them. Maybe she would have sat at the table, and we would have had a nice little 10-minute conversation. But I didn't do that. I was obviously showing impatience; and of course, this MLA role was "oh so important" that I couldn't be late. She told me that she was planning on doing the dishes when I left, and not to worry about them.

Had I known this was the last conversation I would ever have with my mother, who did anything I ever asked of her, my "oh so important" job and my need to get to a meeting on time would have been put in check. My ego was squarely checked when I returned to her apartment. She was already gone, and the smell of death lingered in her apartment. I looked at her dishes; they were washed and neatly stacked on the counter to dry. I have never felt so small. That changed me forever. I learned to check my ego, because you just never know what significant task or statement will be the one that plants a seed of regret. Bulletproof yourself from regret at all costs; it's the most painful bullet to take.

Bulletproofing yourself takes discipline. Don't ignore the signs. When you feel like you're force feeding yourself affirmations that don't fit, when you experience exhaustion, when your mind becomes fuzzy, and you forget your own child's name, this is a sign that you've got to protect the base that you've built, or soon you will be at risk of taking steps backwards.

Be cognizant of these signs. No one is asking you to be perfect or to feel happy and free all the time. But what you need to keep at the centre of your outward gaze, is discipline. That means protecting your physical body first, and allowing the biology of healthy habits, like we saw in Steps 4 and 6, to remain strong. If you let go of the required tenacity to keep up healthy practices and routines, you'll see that you will be sent back to the "start square" in the game of life.

I've read that even choosing a physical stance, like a superhero, and doing this for 2 minutes, will raise hormone levels, like testosterone, and decrease cortisol, which is the stress hormone released to stimulate the sympathetic response. I say, why not do this every once in a while, at the very least for fun! But the strongest way of protecting what you've built is to work those high-performance muscles so that they stay consistently in a state where positive affirmations, envisioning success, and other very simple strategies will continue to have an effect. This is about being consistent, setting appropriate boundaries, and remaining on course.

One way to ensure you remain disciplined is to create a vision board. I know, this seems very cliché to you if you've seen it being done every new year, as a resolution. But look at it this way. It's like sharpening the saw. It's not hard to do. It shows that you take care of

Step 7 – Becoming Bullet Proof

yourself so that you can perform at your optimum, and it's an activity that can be enjoyable as well. There's something about the repetitive motion of sharpening a saw that loosens up the mind and promotes creativity. A vision board is like that too. You can get lost in the time, cutting, positioning, and re-positioning your visionary thoughts. You may even find yourself having new and more improved thoughts! And what can make the activity even more enjoyable is to do it with someone else: a spouse, your child, or your own parents!

If you've never done a vision board, here's how:

Reflect on some themes that you think are important to achieving the goals you set in Step 4. Here are some topics you may want to consider:

- Personal Relationships
- Romance
- Travel
- Finances
- Enjoyment & Fun
- Health
- Money
- Spirituality & Personal Growth
- Physical Environment

Using the goals you set in Step 4, and the list of topics above, decide on what you would like to achieve within one year.

Next, choose some images, quotes, or small objects that you can include on your vision board. I like to thumb through magazines because of the kinesthetic benefit I get from it. I also think it helps to focus my thoughts on finding the specific image that will reinforce my goal. This is a great way to train your mind to look for ways to fulfill the image you have of your ultimate end goal.

You can also create a digital vison board, and I've created an example that you can download at RenewYourPurposeToday.com.

Keep in mind that your board should not be cluttered with too many objects and images. This will keep your thoughts about your goals clearer, and help you avoid being overwhelmed, or inviting cluttered thoughts into your mind.

Once you've settled on some images, you can even add 3-D objects to your vision board. These can be found in the scrapbooking section of your local craft supply store. You should also decide what background you'd like to use for your vision board. Again, the craft supply store will have a variety of choices for you. It can be a pin board, tri fold, photo frame, or other creative idea that you decide! The possibilities are only limited by your imagination!

Begin to place the images and objects, and quotes or messages on your chosen board. Once you've decided how you'd like to place the images, affix them to the board. You can use a variety of tools to do this. I like to use a low temperature glue gun if I know that I won't have to re-affix my images and objects. You can choose other tools as well, like staples, tape, pins, thumbtacks, glue, or whatever matches the style, as well as your personal preference.

When your board is assembled, place it in a location that you'll see often. You can bring it to your workplace if that's appropriate. Setting it on a frame on your bedside table can also be a great way to remind yourself to stay disciplined and focused on your goals.

The experience of making a vision board will unleash your inner creativity. In so many ways, this small gesture can really be beneficial and help bulletproof your goal setting. It will increase your focus by being a physical reminder of your commitments, as well as provide a sense of purpose for you to explore subconsciously.

Step 7 – Becoming Bullet Proof

You've come a long way by now! By putting Steps 1 to 7 into action, you've taken yourself on a journey that may have begun with self-doubt. In Steps 1 and 2, you learned to take responsibility for your actions and began a healing process. This helped strengthen your faith in yourself as a human who can grow, and improve by learning from the past. You've used the practices in Step 3 to set a solid foundation for yourself to rebuild healthy emotional and psychological constructs. Your physical body has started to feel stronger and more agile as well. Reflections, and the thoughts you're having, are starting to become clearer, and your purpose is beginning to form. This foundation opened the door to being able to set goals and create a plan to achieve your greatest wishes! You've also prepared yourself for any setbacks, by altering your mindset and recognizing that it takes time to do big things. And as you continue to pursue your goals, you can see that discipline plays a major role in keeping your mind and body ready for action. Small routines in your day have become not just a part of your schedule; they are a part of your character. This chapter, Step 7, has given you some additional tools to protect the hard work you've done up to this point, and you are already on your way in your renewal of your purpose.

You're really there! Step 8! The final step is like the icing on a cake. You create abundance by preparing yourself as you just have! You will know that what you've worked so hard to achieve is working, because you will feel as though luck, wealth, fortune, and love are all coming to you. When this prosperity starts to flow, you will naturally have the desire to give. This is such a beautiful action, and it acts like a pebble in a still pond by activating a ripple effect. You want to activate your purpose for one simple reason. You want to change the world for the better. We all do. And the next chapter and final step is about enjoying the fruits of your labour. Let's go and reap the harvest!

Chapter 9
Step 8 – Giving Back

*"When a gift is difficult to give away,
it becomes even more rare and precious,
somehow gathering a part of the giver to the gift itself."*
— Cate Blanchett

I believe that there are 4 types of giving:

1. Giving your best
2. Giving to yourself
3. Giving to others
4. Giving to the universe

Giving Your Best

There are many religions and theological or spiritual groups that have traditions that require people to bring the ripest fruits or the richest harvest wheat and lay it on an altar. When I've seen this in my travels, I have to admit that I was a little confounded. I didn't see the purpose of leaving perfectly good food on an altar to wither away. Now I understand the deep message of this action. I realize that it's about giving our best; not just giving an object, but bringing our best self to the table of life.

When you complete your 8-step journey, you will know it, because your mind is right now saying to you that it's prepared to bring the best YOU forward. It's time to praise yourself for doing the hard work that will now enable you to bring your renewed purpose and actualize it. Yes, give back to yourself by acknowledging the path you've just taken. It was not easy, but one step at a time, what you just did was to give your level best. You gave yourself oxygen, nourishment of the body, mind, and soul. You gave yourself peace, through forgiveness and acceptance. All of the steps you've just covered were all crafted to help you realize that when you give to yourself, you can live big. It is the only way to be able to live your dreams.

Giving to Yourself

You now know what giving yourself the best feels like. Turn that feeling into a permanent part of your everyday life. Make no apologies for giving yourself the freedom to serve yourself. Use a calendar, wake up early, and give yourself the best slice of the day! People will adapt around your behaviours, and learn that for you to give them your best, you must maintain your disciplined approach. Just like on a flight, the attendants always tell the passengers that in the event of the aircraft pressure changing, an oxygen mask will automatically drop down. This book was that oxygen mask dropping down. You did exactly as you needed to have done. The flight attendant also stresses that before putting the mask on children or others in your care, you put it on yourself first. By going through each of these steps, you've done just that, and now you're ready to give back to the world.

Giving to Others

You're now ready to share your purpose with others. This is embedded in the goals you've set for yourself, and the changes that you've made to your mindset. Not only are you up, you're ready to go, and you are going to be giving your very best to those you serve. Yes, we are all here to serve. The act of service to others is our gift to them, but it is also our gift to ourselves. The feeling of love, and the release that is like freedom when we give, is priceless. Just think about when you give someone a present. You've taken the time to find the right item that will bring a smile to the face of the receiver. Your delight is in watching their face light up in surprise, joy, and excitement. This seems to be universally true of human beings. I remember every Christmas, as a teacher, the students would bring in gifts. They would usually run up to me with pride and want to know when I would open their gift. Even when I taught teenagers. Especially when I taught teenagers! Some classes wanted and thoroughly enjoyed watching their teacher open gifts at the end of the last day before Christmas. They would repeatedly ask me to open these gifts, and though I worried that some would feel left out, I eventually realized that it was important for them to see the effects of giving. I, of course, made a fuss over each gift, and gave each student a unique expression of my gratitude. Giving to others is actually sometimes better than receiving, I've found. When you are in a position of being able to share because you've created a life of abundance, it's an even greater feeling.

Giving to the Universe

For some of you, the universe may be God. For others, another spiritual entity, and for others still, a galaxy beyond or an energetic field. If you don't believe in an alternate source of guidance, you may alter this type of giving as you see fit.

I believe that God has created each of us towards a specific purpose. We each play an important role in an infinitely intersecting set of patterns. Our actions towards one another become like the sharing of energy, constantly turning, harmonizing, creating balance, flowing, and creating an expansion of love and mutual support that will enable you to get to a place of peace, which is finding your true purpose. This changes, and we adapt in concert with the people and the circumstances around us. But giving to the universe is a powerful, almost mystical phenomenon. It is the source of the title of this book. When we align ourselves with the universe around us, we are able to perceive and believe, and that is *meaningful.*

There is something else to add to giving. And without this, giving would be meaningless. It's being thankful, which amounts to receiving. If you cannot graciously receive, you will feel lonely, alone, and even empty. The way to fully relate to one another is to complete the circle of giving by receiving. When someone holds a door open for you, and you thank them, this is an example of completing the circle. There is

Step 8 – Giving Back

a short and small connection that transpires between people, and it also creates a ripple effect. We call this paying it forward. I experienced this on a walk along a wooded trail on the first day of the New Year. I was alone and was taking in the beauty of the sunlight sparkling on the snow, the scampering squirrels, and other such outdoorsy sights. I was feeling very upbeat, and it must have shown in my face because the others along the trail began spontaneously wishing me a Happy New Year. I liked this! I began doing the same to others, and it was as though we were all enjoying this gorgeous day as a group of friends. The energy was so special that I will always fondly remember that day.

It was special, you see, because I shared and showed appreciation. Showing others that you're thankful or grateful has an exponential effect on their performance. Within organizations where there is a culture of bullying or fear, this appreciation has slowly been whittled away by pervasive criticism, and then fear of being criticized. When I do work with organizations that show this type of corporate culture, it is almost always related to lack of visibility of the leader. Added to this, the leader is often perceived as being present, only to reprimand or find fault. When this is the case, it's difficult to find a pathway to reconciliation. In fact, it is only possible if the leader is able to approach a rebuild of the culture in the same way as you have approached the steps of this book. If you are the leader of a corporation, bear this message in mind: Gratitude is a characteristic of the greatest leaders. Don't forget to pause and give thanks publicly, and especially privately, and also mean it.

Generosity is another part of Step 8, Giving Back. When you reap the harvest of your good work, your financial goals will also begin to materialize. When this happens, you should find opportunities to save for a rainy day—maybe treat yourself to a vacation or some other form of celebrating your success. Also, remember that offerings to those in need is an important form of giving. I have turned this into my own private deposits that are unseen by others. The recipient doesn't need to know, and you don't need to receive recognition for this type of giving. In fact, even before your financial boon arrives, there are many ways to express this kind of generosity. Check out this list, and add some of your own!

- As you clean out the clutter from your space, prepare clothing and other valuable items you no longer use, to give up for donation. This will not only clear your space and clear your mind; you will be fulfilling a need for someone else.

- Choose a non-profit organization that aligns with your values. Throughout the year, put away an amount that you can send to this organization quarterly. They will be financially better off, but you are also establishing a new, positive connection and relationship. When you are ready, volunteer for this organization. You will be rewarded ten-fold.

- Send thank you notes by mail to people you do business with, to your child's teacher, and to the manager of the local grocery store. This small action will change someone's day, and when you put that card or note in the mail, it will give you a boost of dopamine!

- Give freely and without expectation. If you expect to receive something in return, or if you calculate your giving for the purpose of balancing your generosity, you will indeed accumulate debt in the form of bitterness and envy.

- Tip your favourite restaurant staff randomly when you aren't dining in the restaurant. The act of showing appreciation, by dropping off a $100 bill for the staff to put towards enjoying drinks on the patio, will be remembered. I believe that this type of generosity is returned to me multiplied.

- When you pass homeless people and don't offer money, always offer them a smile and a warm greeting.

Step 8 – Giving Back

- Your neighbourhood schools fundraise for non-essentials and those students in need. At the beginning of the school year, bring a backpack with new school supplies to your local school.

- Each time you go grocery shopping, make a point of selecting a couple items to drop into the food bank bin on your way out. It's a great feeling to add special items to this bin, like a box of cake mix that may just make someone a very happy birthday!

- Shovel your neighbour's sidewalk. You'll find that this is one task on your list that you'll be cutting in half, because they will likely be very happy to do the same in return. And if they don't, do it anyway. You don't know what is going on in someone's life, and the simple gesture of taking on a task like this, may be a big, positive difference in their day.

- Give a stranger a compliment. Looking for something to notice and show gratitude for in a stranger, is a great way to acknowledge the good things around you.

- Leave a sticky note with a loving message for your child or your spouse, on their mirror. You will probably notice that they leave it there to enjoy for some time after you place it.

- Send a personal note to commend someone, on one of your social media profiles, for an award they've recently received, or an accomplishment that they have made.

- Set aside a small budget to buy a coffee card once a week. Present it to someone you meet that may need a pick-me-up!

- Pay it forward at the pump. Fill up a stranger's heart by fueling their gas tank. Just let the attendant at your neighbourhood service station know that you'd like to pay for someone's gas.

- In the spring and summer, when you see winter clothing like gloves and socks on sale, buy them, and put them away until the next winter. Send them to the local homeless shelter before the first big snowfall of the year.

By performing these displays of gratitude, you are giving to people in need. You, too, will be in need of this same kind of compassion delivered with sincerity. But most of all, it just feels good to be able to offer someone a hand up when they need it most.

Giving back reminds you that you have something to be grateful for, and it reinforces the work you've put in to be able to become successful. It doesn't have to be material either. The fruit of your labour is sweeter when shared with others.

This reminds me! I promised to return to the topic of postulation. Postulation is a great way to end step 8. It's a powerful mindset that allows you to manifest great things in your life. All the examples of giving above are actions I freely do because I believe in creating space in my life for receiving abundance. This is an example of how to achieve postulation.

It is complicated and simple at the same time. It's complicated because all the 8 steps need to be actively engaged in a sort of synergy. In my opinion, postulation doesn't work if you don't have clarity, belief and love. But, when you've worked on the 8 steps you'll achieve these and will notice how miracles seem to align themselves in your favour. Obstacles move out of the way by your own ability to think clearly. Belief allows you to see the next step instead of being overwhelmed by the prospect of eating the whole elephant. You appreciate love in your relationships and in your surroundings. This creates a whole strengthened physical system in your body, it heightens your senses in a healthy manner, you hear and see things more clearly. Some people call it intuition, a 6th sense, clairvoyance and so on. My belief is that an alignment between our physical, mental, emotional and spiritual

Step 8 – Giving Back

state occurs when you can truly perform these 8 steps. It leads you to that 100% mark of being unstoppable and turns into as close to a superpower as you can get. That is postulation and it's POWERFUL. Use it. But most of all, respect it. This means staying disciplined and not straying so far away from your promises that you get lost on the mountain. Discipline is truly the one concept that supersedes everything. It's the will over all your thoughts and actions and it's your Sherpa that will guide you back to Base Camp when you begin to get lost!

And how exciting that we've gone through the 8 steps and you are now looking back at the person who started this journey 100 days ago. Celebrate this accomplishment and store it into your album of memoires. It's your re-birthday!

Chapter 10
Happy Re-Birthday!

"To accomplish great things, we must not only act but also dream; not only plan but also believe."
— Anatole France

www.RenewYourPurposeToday.com

10

By now, you've really noticed changes in yourself physically, emotionally, and spiritually. Your relationships, circumstances, and financial outlook will likely show welcome signs of growth. Take this time to celebrate your achievements. You can do many things to mark this moment of feeling renewed and purposeful. One idea is to schedule a photo shoot and capture the vibrance you are showing right now. You can always use the photos to update your online career portfolio, or turn the shoot into a family photo session. Photos have a way of immortalizing a memory. And now that you are seeing your own light and purpose, framing that image of yourself in an actual frame also sets it into your mental framework.

If a photo shoot is not your style, at the very least, do take this opportunity to write yourself a letter. Do it in the third person and acknowledge all that you've accomplished. I recommend even mailing it to yourself and opening that same letter a year from the date you receive it! Another idea is to set a date for sending yourself an email, in your email settings. Remember how, at the beginning of your journey, you looked back in hindsight to what went wrong? You are now going to read a letter, a year from now, and it will be a very real, virtual reminder of all that you did right!

Your letter can look something like this…

Happy Re-Birthday!

Dear Christine,

I know that your journey to renewal felt like a long and tough path. When I look at you today, I can see that every challenge you faced has helped you grow into a more patient, caring, healthy, and self-loving person. It was worth the journey.

Today, you are in the best shape of your life and have found the balance that eluded you for so long. Despite all that you achieved in your adult life, you know that truthfully, you were headed towards danger at the speed you continuously felt you had to maintain. It's as though when that right turn presented itself, and you spun out and crashed, you were forced to take a look at what important changes needed to happen for you to be whole again. You did the necessary work to make this healing and renewal happen. You took your physical health seriously, and added some really great routines to maintain all that you worked for.

The resting that you took was much needed, and you deserved to be able to take some time to heal, improve, and grow into the new person you see in the mirror today. You are loving, caring, smart, and tenacious, and you have an inner power that is being unleashed to do good in this world...

You get the idea. The more personal and specific you make your letter to yourself, the more value you'll get out of it in the future.

Remember that you will likely encounter small and even serious setbacks in the future. But you've now been able to set yourself a course of action to mitigate the long-term effects that a downturn in your life can have.

The most significant principle in all that you've learned in the "8 Steps to Renew Your Purpose," is to be disciplined. If you can consistently keep yourself in a state of high-level performance, all else can almost *meaningfully* fall into alignment. It's what high achievers, successful businesspeople, and professional athletes do. That's why they stand out. They are outliers. Outliers know they are onto something good, and they don't concern themselves with the impossibilities. From now on, be an outlier.

Outliers see the light, and they find a way to get more of that light to shine on them and their ideas. Think of your life as a light seeker. Seeds are light seekers. Think about it. A tiny little seed gets buried in the dirt, and somehow that seed finds its way to the light.

Just like you have done, that seed managed to grow, despite being buried in the dark earth. Even as it was planted in the dirt, it may have even been trampled upon, not been watered for some time and gotten no sun. But that seed was destined to provide something to the earth no matter what. Just like you. You are on this Earth to provide something important to others, and make meaning for yourself—to serve a purpose. For that seed, it may become a flower, a fern, or even a large oak tree. It will only reach its destiny by nourishment from the soil, even if sometimes that nourishment is manure! Sure, it stinks sometimes. But life is just sometimes like that.

Your time will always follow dark times. That seed may have to wait patiently, resting in the soil. It may even have to wait many seasons for the rain to finally pour down and cause it to wake. But when it receives the cleansing rainfall, it begins to stir. That seed begins to build stronger inside its shell. When the rain continues to nourish it, the seed starts to grow, and even sprouts! And somehow that seed knows how to reach up. It's just so natural that it must be something you can trust, as much as the sun setting and rising each day. As the seed becomes a sprout, it pushes through the darkness, where it was resting and building up strength. And when the first green leaf peeks from the dirt, that leaf is vulnerable and sensitive to the conditions

Happy Re-Birthday!

above ground. But it's also resilient, full of nutrients, and ready to accept the comfort of the sun. It begins to open its leaves or petals to take in the world around it.

If this sounds familiar, it should. The same miraculous journey that every seed takes, so does every soul. So, rest assured that you are meant to succeed and achieve your wildest dreams. The conditions here on Earth are all set up for you to do this. You just have to first make the decision to take the steps, and then commit yourself to trusting the journey.

I hope that this book has made a difference for you. Yes, I wrote it so you would find comfort, because that can be so hard to find when we are struggling. Beyond that, I wish for you to find peace and joy in the life that you truly deserve.

Please check out my site regularly for the latest updates, free material, workshops, and upcoming webinars, where you can meet others who are also on their own journey to renewing their purpose.

RenewYourPurposeToday.com